CW00952915

www.united-pc.eu

BEATRICE FINN

EILEEN

A Mayo Girl With Professional Inspirations

Acknowledgements

A very special "Thank You" to my friend Diane Jarvis. Without your help and encouragement I would not have this achievement

A heartfelt tribute to my late parents, Pakie Finn and Mary Ann Finn nee Forkin. You gave us your children the enviable experience of life in the countryside, in the bogs of Cloontia and off the grid. Albeit living off the grid was never a choice for you.

You gave us the inspiration to be the best we could be in life. Jointly we hope that you would both approve of the content of Eileen

We love and miss you both

Table Of Contents

Continued

Memory Lane

A few small villages all clustered together, where most people knew each other and were part of each other's lives'. Most families had around five children . Some had as many as eleven or even twelve. We had the usual public house, a small shop, post office, a school and of course a church and a graveyard. All of the homes were built from stone, were single story, had a thatched roof and consisted of no more than probably two rooms in total. None would have had a bathroom, so the rest is left to the imagination. Of course, toilet paper was a piece from the Sunday Herald or some grass leaves which ever was the closest. A river flowed at the end of our meadow, shallow in parts deep in others. It was 1927. Cloontia with its narrow lanes, borrens, bogs and hay fields had always felt like a nice place to be.

It was hard to decide how the day was going to turn out, weather wise I mean. The sky looked a bit gloomy. It was cold outside. Raindrops fell gently on the roof tops, glistening from time to time as the sunshine occasionally broke through. There was no sunshine in my heart. I wanted to scream, to scream at our God, but I knew that it wouldn't make the slightest bit of difference. Ask and you shall receive! How many times had I heard that statement? Well I asked. I asked for my husband to be cured. It didn't happen. The sight of John, laying there, his body rigid and cold as ice. He was dead. Stony cold dead .He had died almost in front of my eyes. The unfairness of it all. That's a picture that I will never forget. My John, strong John, who in many ways, was the rock in our marriage and then he had gone. Gone and left me by myself. The grand nurse from Donegal, who had looked after him, came over to the bed. She had a look of discomfort about her. Pneumonia she said, with a quiver in her voice. There was nothing more that we could have done. He was reasonably comfortable, like that was going to help me at that time. She touched my hand. She knew how I was feeling. The poor woman had been in my shoes only two years previous. She had previously shared with me that her husband of many years, had dropped dead ,in front of her and her children, as he was walking through the door to go down to the farm. Her being a nurse as well, yet there was nothing she could do to save him. She wondered if she could help me in any other way and then went back to her desk. I think she was feeling lonesome for me. She had that look of compassion in her eyes. I held Johns hand for what seemed like an eternity, in the same way that he squeezed my hand on our wedding day. This was one of the very few times, that I had that psychical contact with John ,the man I had been married to for many years and now he wasn't here to realise I was holding his hands. Suddenly I was overwhelmed with guilt. Why hadn't I done that before? Why had I always waited to let John be the one to take my hand? Why oh Why? Tears began to roll down my face. The nurse came back she took my arm

"Come on Biddy its time you went home"

I didn't want to go home. I didn't want to leave my John in that place. My world had crashed down before my eyes. How could it have happened? What was god thinking about when he allowed this to happen to us? Here in this small village, in County Mayo, in the West of Ireland , holy Catholic Ireland, where everyone lived by the word of God, where we said our daily prayers on bended knees, and then out of the blue, our lives were destroyed in a moment of time. That was what happened to other people, not to my family. How would I get through the rest of my life without the man I loved? What would I tell my little girls, and how would they cope without their daddy? The journey home from Castlebar was a highly emotional one. As the bus churned its way through the villages I reminisced of all the times myself and John had made that journey together over the years. I remembered how he would scowl at, and about, the youngsters who were what seemed to be forever hanging about doing nothing. The bus arrived back in Ballaghaderreen. The reality of the whole situation was building up in my head. I had to take a car from Ballagh to the house. It was almost dark. I put the besom with a white sheet draped over it by the front door. That was my signal to the girls to come home. A neighbour had looked after them for the day. The day that would be better if it never came to an end. I made a strong pot of tea and ate a little soda bread. I knew that I had to keep strong. What I really needed was a large glass of punch strong enough to calm my nerves. Sweat was pouring from my forehead. I trembled from head to toe. The girls came running across the meadow. Talking and laughing with each other. They had stopped at the river for a few minutes. I wondered if they were looking for trout. The closer they got the faster I trembled. As they approached the front door I think that they guessed from the look on my face that something awful had happened.

"Jaysus mammy what's happened? What's wrong? Is Daddy all right? Mammy say something talk to us, talk to us"

We hugged each other for a few seconds and then I gave them the news that shattered their lives. I barely managed to get the words out. The three of us stood there shaking. I knew I had to console myself in order to keep my children consoled. We sat together for what seemed like an eternity. So many questions to be answered. So many plans to be made. The days leading up to the funeral were very dismal. John's body was returned back to the house. It remained there for 5 days. Relations came from England. People came and went, showing their respect and making offers of

"Shall I bake soda bread for you Biddy"?

Soda bread! Why did everyone think that soda bread would make things all right? I wanted something that would take my feelings away, take away the hurt from my broken heart. Give my husband back to me! Take away the pain from my children's faces. The reality of the situation was staring at me and I knew that I was being unreasonable in my reaction to the offers of soda bread. We got through the following days, however looking back I'm not sure how. The girls, and especially Eileen, demonstrated a maturity beyond their years, right up to the day of the funeral, when Kathy our youngest daughter, screamed all morning. We tried to keep her busy handing out cigarettes. Kathy did like the attention she was getting from everyone. She missed her daddy too, and struggled to understand, why, and how, she had lost him. Eileen, always the comforter, always putting others before herself, even as a small child decided to take charge of the situation. She spoke the words with a gentleness that only she possessed

"Sure you're a grand girl Kathy, go and help Mammy put the tea out "

Eileen, even at that young age, was aware that her sister was struggling more than she was. Eileen wanted to help, and felt that the best way to do that was to keep Kathy busy. The morning went fast, till eventually, it was time to go. The procession was long. John had been a much loved, by everyone type of man. They came from the adjoining villages to say their goodbyes. Local men carried the coffin, the whole four miles to the church, interchanging with each other along the way. The Mass seemed to go on forever, and then, the final part of the journey to the Graveyard, where he was laid to rest. A few of the old ones came back home with us. They shared the few bottles John had put aside for a special day. This wasn't how he planned it. This wasn't the idea of the special day for supping his stout.

Of course, the years have gone by since those days, and never in a million of them, did I imagine what the future held in store for our family. We had two beautiful daughters who would have very different lives. They endured struggles, tragedy, love and hate and brought new meanings to all of my days.

I had a big stretch on my bed before deciding what to do next. It was one of those days. You know. The sort where you just have to do, what you have to do. I was up at the crack of dawn. The ducks quacking away in the yard, as if to say where is breakfast then , and spot the old sheep dog, restless in his bed, all contributed to stopping me from sleeping. Morning Prayer was the first thing on my mind, I would pray for a real nice warm dry day. The turf needed cutting and you couldn't do that unless the weather was dry. I had breakfast. A rasher of bacon with a freshly laid egg, and some soda bread, followed by a long walk to collect some water from the well. The buckets were real heavy, when full of water. I decided to take just one, and then I could swap over when my hands started to ache. Walking down that meadow to the well, brought back thoughts, and feelings, I would prefer not to remember. Once I was back home with the water I made myself some tea, and sat staring out of the window. The sun began to shine through the branches of the trees. The village was still asleep; the world seemed like a nice place to be. I was on my own and in a reminiscing sort of mood. I decided that I hadn't been over the yard for a long time and wondered how it might feel to go there. When I arrived at the old doorway, I froze on the spot. My thoughts were very deep, feeling almost as though I had been immersed into some sort of trance or other. I chuntered to myself

"Jesus, Mary and Joseph forgive me"

Me thinking about some trance or other, and me being a good Catholic woman and all that. Trance belongs to those who talk to the dead not people like me. It was a good job that I had a handkerchief tucked away in my pocket. I needed it. I talked to myself giving the sort of advice I usually dished out to others. Pull yourself together Biddy it's all in the past now and life has to go on. The words of wisdom didn't make any difference didn't go any way to changing how I was feeling at that very moment in time. I began to scream inwardly at myself again!

" Jaysus woman will you pull yourself together".

I wiped my tears away; My first thoughts were about John, and how I was wishing that he could see the place now. He wouldn't believe what was in front of his eyes. If only he could see the family and how they had grown. I know that he would be so proud of his daughters, and his grandchildren, and the sort of adults his daughters have turned into. I tried to talk to him, and at the same time wondered if I was going mad. What would he make of Padraig, and the way he lives his life, the way he treats Eileen. Would he appreciate his Kathy being married to Michael Mc Geever? The McGeevers were never John's favourite people. He sort of looked down on them but of course would never admit to that. On market and fair days, the competition between John, and Jimmy McGeever would always be fierce. They would wonder who had produced the biggest cow, the fattest pig. I'm remembering one particular occasion, when John, actually swapped four pigs for a very large cow, with our neighbour. He had heard a rumour that Jimmy's cows were fatter than ours. The silliness of it all, as it was then, but what wouldn't I give to get those days back

"Go away with you John, sure yourself, and Jimmy McGeever are like kids"

But alas, when Jimmy Mc Geever was brought into the conversation, John never heard what I was saying. I was always amazed how his hearing would deteriorate when he choose for that to happen. Thank heavens; our children have grown up, into nicely rounded adults, without those traits. The years have flown by, and things have changed, almost as much as the seasons change, from one year to the next. I wonder what john would make of the spot where I'm standing right now.

The old place is still there. It has a thatched roof, leaking in one corner. The milk churn, now covered in rust, standing in that same place, for years, and years, against the gable wall. Sure I'm amazed how it's still in one piece. Seeing the churn standing there, has brought tears to my eyes, as it's a reminder of the olden days, and watching my own mother collect the milk daily in preparation for the churning of the butter, then sending the leftovers to the creamery in Ballaghaderreen. Geary's tractor came to the bridge every Thursday morning to collect the churns. Six pence to a shilling was the usual reward from the creamery, and of course, if you went into Ballagh with the children you would spend the shilling in no time at all. The ice cream was always so tempting .The plain vanilla sliced off the block, and wedged between two wafers, was favourite for all of us. It was also the most expensive. A small thin wedge cost a penny, a slightly thicker one cost tuppence

"Can we have one mammy?" and how do you say no, especially when that's the only treat the children were likely to receive, till the next visit to the town, which would probably be several weeks away

As kids, we all mucked in with the milking of the cows, and then, seeing the end result in the butter dish was amazing. We often struggled with figuring out how it got from milk, to a solid butter, it's the leprechauns said me Da, they have their magic powers. Isn't it amazing how convincing that could be to a small child? Those were happy days that I will always remember.

The winter had been exceptionally hard, very wet, with lots of snow fall, and freezing temperatures, so, what should I expect, in regard to the roof? What would John think if he could see it now? He loved the homestead, loved working on the land and especially on the area he put down to garden. John spent so many hours working in the garden area, and then having a smoke, and a read of the Western People.

"John are you ever coming inside? Its eleven o clock, it's been a long day and I'm tired."

The usual response from him was one of silence. I don't think that he ever appreciated how much, his behaviour had frustrated me, had sometimes left me feeling cold and unwanted. I often felt envy, when I saw the way, other couples interacted and seemed to be enjoying the company of each other. I often wondered if I had done something wrong, but deep down in my soul I knew that I hadn't. I knew that this was John's personality, his way, however, many a time, a prayer I said on bended knees, in the hope of changing the man that I was married too. Alas, this wasn't going to, and never did happen. John was John and his ways were what made him the person he was. I knew he loved me in his own way. He always, in one way or another, gave strength to our marriage, despite the difficulties we shared.

John would spend all his spare time in the garden plot, lovingly tending to the plants. Every new shoot that appeared would be a challenge for him. Could he nurture it enough to give strong plants the following year? Might there be enough to take to the market and make a few shillings ? John had to have a challenge. To him his gardening was a labour of love. I hated him spending all his spare time that way. Why didn't he want to be with me and the children more? Why didn't he love us as much as he loved his garden? What was it that he had been escaping from? Did his children, our children have any idea of the difficult relationship between their parents? A relationship that didn't need to be so distant, if only, John had thought a little more of others, a little less of himself. I tortured myself with those thoughts, and all of those questions from time to time. I constantly wondered, and sometimes worried if our relationship would have a bad influence on the future relationships of our daughters. Then I consoled myself by reminders that we went to mass every Sunday, as a good Catholic family should do, therefore giving them the feeling of togetherness. After Mass we congregated in the small shop across the road from the Chapel. The girls always had a little money to spend on sweets, whilst John and I got a newspaper and chatted away to the neighbours. We both worked hard on the farm and provided to the best of our ability for our children. I would then convince myself that things couldn't be all that bad, and that they enjoyed more family life than some.

I would sometimes fall into bed at night, exhausted, from the day that had just passed. My pillow would often be wet, from the silent tears that would roll down my face. The girls couldn't know. They couldn't know that their mammy was this lonely, nor know the reason why. When asked to join us John would often protest, telling me that every man needs an interest needs a hobby. I sometimes almost begged for his attention.

"Come and have a game of cards we can play whist"

He wasn't interested! Never showed any affection, never a hug, never a kiss. John was of the opinion that so long as the day's work was done, then I should be happy and content. Physical affection wasn't in his world. I know that in his own way he cared, and that he had a respect for me. My sister would always be at his defence. I often wondered if she had wanted him for herself. I often caught her looking at him in a longing way, and then looking away quickly, when she wasn't noticed by him. John wasn't the sort to look elsewhere. Despite his other short comings, he was a one woman man. Despite my feelings of abandonment by my husband, I was a one man woman. I loved him dearly. My sister would constantly offer reassurance

"Sure that's the way with Irish men Biddy. You're lucky to have met John and he's such a nice man in many ways. You could have been like me; you could have been a lonely old spinster. What would you do then? At least you and John have had the children together and he is a good man. You have the home, and the land, and two beautiful daughters growing up".

My sister simply didn't understand! Her thoughts were, that if the home was kept running, and the children were produced, then what more should anyone want. Maybe that's the reason that she's a spinster. Who would have been attracted to a woman, who was as cold and uncaring as she was?

John came from a very large family. He had seven brothers and four sisters of whom three died at birth. He had always struggled with the fact that as we both were from large families, we ended up, by Irish Catholic standards, having a very small family ourselves. I had suffered six miscarriages, and of course there wasn't any help or intervention . I tried to help John to understand that really we were quite fortunate to have had two children, and would often pray the rosary in gratitude for them.

John was a short man, with a fine head of hair, carrying a few extra pounds in his later years. He smoked woodbines and drank the odd bottle or two of stout. He often made his own Poiton, (Pronounced Puc-Cheen) in the same way as many Irish farmers did, however he didn't especially like the taste. Of course, whilst poiton was traditionally, a drink that belongs to Irish culture, it was illegal to brew . John was an upstanding man, with good principles on the whole, but where the poiton was concerned, he was on the side of the farmer. Together with many other farmers from County Mayo he spent many hours working on this illegal practise. They stacked the barrels side by side behind the house, covering them with straw and hay bales, in case the Garda (police) graced us with an appearance. One of his favourite times of the month, would be on the last Thursday, when his dole money was due. He loved to go to Donovan's in the town, where he shared a couple of bottles with the neighbours, and then up to the grocery shop, where he bought the currant bracks that we all loved so much. John often wondered why I couldn't bake a currant brack myself. I wondered too, as I always baked the soda bread, which was a big part of our daily dietary habit. John was always up early, and went to bed late. A hard working man, who expected others to be the same, and had no patience with those who were different,

"Sure Jimmy Mc Geever would lie in bed all day long"

That would be John's favourite description of Jimmy when he felt the need to have a go. Johns chair is now empty, and rusting behind the barns. Oh God how much I miss him, no one will ever know. It's been many a long, lonely year, since we put him in the ground.

The New House

This is our daughter's house. The very second that I walk through the front door, I can feel the presence of John, he belongs here, especially in the parlour where his picture sits proudly. I can sense his shadow in every room that I walk into. I can feel his presence in the garden like he's watching over it, in the way that he always did. I have to go behind the barns to sit on his rusty chair. I talk to him, quietly sharing our daughters life's, sharing all my worries, and asking him to intercede where Padraigs concerned. Even though I can't see him, I can feel his presence. I know that he's there, with me, by that chair, in the silent way that belongs to him. And no I'm not going into a trance I'm using my imagination and maybe playing a game of pretend. I don't know, it feels real to me and is so very comforting. Some would say and in particular my older sister that I am simply a foolish old woman, who's wishing for what can never be. I say that every person should do what feels right for them, and if my sister thinks that I'm foolish, and probably thinks that I'm mad, then she can live with those thoughts.

It's a beautiful house, with a slated roof and two chimney stacks, set in several acres of meadow land. The meadows produce so much hay year after year. Again I have fond memories from childhood, of raking the hay together with my father, and then making the stacks before the rain came. That was always a gamble with the good old Irish climate.

The walled garden at the front of the new house is full of bloom, from deep red rose bushes, and purple Hyacinths, which have been planted there for several years. Before his death, John had planted the hedgerow, on what is now the gable side, with an overgrown area which is a delight to the local wildlife. Many times we have found a tiny little egg on the ground, that's fallen from the nest that has been so carefully put together by the birds. The porcupine and hedgehogs have been seen sneaking up close to the front door, to get a drink of milk. I often tell my grandchildren (Yes there's three of them) that if they sit quietly, in the far corner of the wild area, it would be amazing what they might see and hear.

Scent from the wild flowers in the hedgerow is hypnotic. My favourite, is probably in the late spring time when the petunias come into blossom. The children sometimes pick the flowers to take to the church on a Sunday morning. There are some steps going up the long pathway leading to the solid Oak door, with a bay window on each side. Robins, and swallows are nesting in the tall trees that surround the house. On some occasions, when Eileen had found the tiny eggs that have fallen from the nests, she had climbed back up the tree to put them where they belong. On other occasions, the children would get excited and ask

"Will we have them for breakfast mammy?"

Eileen could only ever see the funny side of all that, as the eggs were so tiny. Still she played the game.

Four barns, a pig house and hay shed are built on the west side of the house, whilst Paradig stores his tractor, and other farm equipment, in one very large store at the back of the house. My Grand children spend many hours, together, sometimes with their friends in the fenced in play area, which has a small homemade swing set in the trees, and a pond which has been covered over, never to be used. The children long to have a dip on the warm summer days, but know that it's forbidden.

" Please daddy, it's so hot, sure what harm can it do?"

Seamus, the oldest of them, would demonstrate his level of frustration, by screaming and shouting, and banging his head needlessly until it hurt, and on occasions breaking the skin and drawing blood. It fell on deaf ears; He thought that this level of behaviour would be enough to change his father's mind. It wasn't enough; his feelings about this were never taken on board. Padraig had made his mind up, about how it was going to be, and nothing on this earth was going to move him. He would sometimes come into his Sons face with a look of fury and rage

"Seamus will you give over. How many times do I have to tell you, you can't go in there! "

Padraig never gave a thought to how the child was suffering. He would always be impatient, at times screaming his response to his children. Seamus felt the unfairness of it all, he was disappointed and would protest to me.

"Grandma, please grandma, speak to my daddy "

"No Seamus I can't interfere. It's your father's decision and I have to abide by it too. I cannot go against your father's wishes".

I also, felt the unfairness of it all, but had to keep those thoughts to myself. I wondered if Padraig and Eileen would ever change their view on the upbringing of their children. I also wondered how much of this was Padraigs sole decision, and my daughter didn't have a choice. Padraig was a very domineering character. Eileen would have found it hard to go against him even if she wanted to, and especially, in a situation as serious as this one.

This rambling house, with its five large bedrooms, displays a large plaque on the inside of the porch, showing* Caed Mila Failte*, and a picture of the last supper, in pride of place in the hallway. Rosary Beads, that have been passed down through the generations in our family, are draped over a chair. There's a water font filled with holy water, to bless yourself as you enter the house. This gets replenished when someone has had a visit to Knock Shrine. Bacon and cabbage, is simmering away in the pot, which hangs above the open turf fire. The traditional Irish dinner is something that we have enjoyed for what seems like eternity, and it's all come from the land. The local farmers forever working hard to produce sufficiently in order to maintain their homes and their families. Turf from the bog, is smouldering in the fireplace, casting a beautiful glow throughout the room, with a scent that you would recognise anywhere, or at least an Irish person brought up in the countryside would recognise. There were three oil lamps lit. They were hanging from the ceiling. There were two lanterns hanging, one each side of the front door, casting shadows down the path.

The main rule of the house is that * Each night the family are together, on bended knees, to proclaim their love for the Lord.* Sundays, holydays, would see the pews in the old chapel being graced with their presence. The chapel has stood here for more than 200 years. It is like any typical Roman Catholic Chapel you might come across. It was walking distance from our house, approximately three miles away. It has a large concreted area at one side, looking something almost like a small school playground. The area is rarely used for parking as there are few motor cars throughout the local villages. The concreted area has been well used by the missionary Nuns who regularly set up their stalls to sell their religious artefacts. The church has seen many a family through the generations being raised as devout and staunch Roman Catholics. Weddings, funerals and baptisms, with confession on a Saturday morning followed by communion and Mass every Sunday, have been the events here over the years. Myself and John were married in this very church with just fourteen people present. I was so happy on that day. I walked the long walk to the chapel wearing my new dress, and some flat shoes, that I found in the sale in Corrigan's shoe shop in Ballagh. John's younger brother paid me all the compliments I never got from my new husband

"Jaysus you're a beautiful bride Biddy. Johns a lucky man "

John squeezed my hand tightly, like he would never let me go. After the wedding, we walked the three miles back home in the rain and the rest of our lives together began. We had many a good year together before I experienced what was probably the worst day of my life. That was the day my husband died, the day that my world to some extent came to an end.

The way of life here for Padraig and Eileen, and with the religious aspects of it in particular, you might imagine it, being the perfect scenes to create a blissful and harmonious family home, but then as we discover, things aren't always as they seem

By gone days had seen many a set dance within these walls, as Padraig and Eileen had yet again opened their door to the local musician, put on their hornpipe shoes, and so the fun would begin. The joy of life for them was immense, as they, together with friends, family and neighbours from afar would dance the nights away. House dances, were, and still are a way of life.

Our Daughters

Eileen, as a small child, amongst many other things had learned how to do traditional Irish dancing .Her coordination was never as good as her brain, so learning the different steps for the reels and jigs was something that she struggled with. Her dance teacher assured me, that we shouldn't give up, that once she got the hang of it, she would be off like grease lightning. Money was really scarce, so when we were asked to put Eileen into the Feis(Irish dancing competition pronounced   fesh) that would be happening in a few months time, we had to think about it very hard. The traditional dancing costume, together with the shoes, would cost more than we could afford. John decided that we should sell a cow that we had been saving for the fair the following year. That's how we provided the money for the costume. It was all worthwhile in the end. Winning 2nd place at the National Feis was a surprise to all of us, and in particular to Eileen

"Jaysus mammy I can't believe it. I'm being called back onto the stage to receive a medal".

Eileen's school friends had come to watch the competition. Most were happy for her, one or two were a little jealous and showed this by their comments of

"well doesn't she look the silly one, in the stupid green frock with shamrock all over it, and the thick black shoes"

Eileen ignored their comments. My husband had been as amazed as I was, and of course so proud of our clumsy daughter, with her two left feet. Fourteen lessons before she eventually got the hang of things, got the co- ordination right. Her dance teacher was always very reassuring. After the tenth lesson she told me

"Don't worry Mrs O Hara she will get there eventually"

As usual Eileen was modest. She would never allow the medal to be displayed.

"I know that I've got it mammy. Why do others need to know"?

The medal was pushed into a drawer, and as far as I know, it's still in that same place today. Eileen constantly dismissed any suggestions that she might go places with her dancing. Her teacher had different opinions, and different ideas. She recognised talent when it was staring her in the face. The letter arrived four months later. Eileen had been entered into further competitions to be held in Sligo, if she wished to compete, and if, as her parents, we wished to allow this to happen. The competitions would always be held at the weekend so the children didn't lose time from school. Kathy wasn't interested in the dancing bit. Had it meant time off from school, she may have wanted to participate, as school wasn't her favourite place. She was always anxious to watch her sister perform though. Kathy would beam with excitement, and would always like to exaggerate the situation. She was a bit of a drama queen and very proud of her sister.

"Jaysus Eileen you're so good, your legs are nearly as high as the moon, when you're doing the double Jig "

John, and I, agreed that Eileen could compete if she wished to do so. It would be Eileen's choice. We never believed in pushing the children in any particular direction. Eileen was excited at the idea of going to Sligo.

" Will I need another new costume mammy"?

She practised her dancing every day without music. Just humming to herself in her head. She could remember the tunes very well. Once every week she went to a neighbour's house where she practised the reels and jigs to the sound of the flute. Over, and over, for at least two hours, she would dance away till her legs were so tired that she couldn't go on any more. Competition time arrived. Eileen was well prepared. Some she lost, mostly she won, but always had her modest outlook. This was most obvious when the local newspaper wanted to take a photograph of Eileen, in her dancing costume, holding up the medals which she had just won. She protested to me

"Mammy I won't do it. I don't like it "

This competition in County Sligo brought even more possible success for her. She was seen by an American agent who was looking for promising Irish dancers, to go to New York with all expenses paid. I couldn't believe that he wanted Eileen to join his group. We wondered if it would be the right thing for our daughter. The summer holidays were coming up, so the loss of education wasn't going to be a problem. Even at the age of ten, she was assertive about what she wished to happen for herself, and would present her feelings with a maturity far beyond her years. Eileen had overheard the conversation. The thought of America excited her. We asked for a couple of weeks to think about it. The local and National newspapers were represented at the Feis. They wanted photographs of Eileen and a write up of her dancing achievements. The journalist tried to use bribery but Eileen was not to be manipulated.

"Be off with you I don't want my photograph to be taken. I don't want to appear in the papers, or be on the radio, or anything else. Give the books to another child; well go on then, because I don't want them".

The journalist was very surprised by the reaction from such a young child

"Be Jaysus Mrs O Hara, you have a stubborn one there".

I didn't think that Eileen was stubborn. I considered that she was a private child who knew her own mind and that this maturity would take her places in life. I apologised to the journalist for what he probably considered to be rudeness as well as stubbornness. We took our daughter home. There was three weeks to make a decision on the New York invitation. We talked a lot to Eileen about how she felt. She decided that although she loved her dancing, she didn't wish to leave Ireland and her family at such a young age. I've often wondered how it might have worked out if she had gone.

As a very small child, Eileen was always asking questions about the animals and how their bodies work. She would sit down beside me at the table and have her question and answer time whilst the other children played.

" Mammy how do the chickens lay their eggs? Where do they come from?" was one of the many questions that she would ask. Sometimes it would be difficult to find an explanation for such a young child. John was no help. He always told her,"go ask your mammy".

Eileen had always looked forward to those sessions. She would watch the pigs with intensity when they chased each other round the yard. I could imagine her mind ticking over. Being raised on a farm developed her sense of curiosity around the animals. Developed her interest in the scientific world. She had a good brain, and one day, hopefully would put it to good use. She did like the animals, but as an adult this wasn't where her interest lay.   Everyone who knew Eileen, quiet, reserved, studious, Eileen, except Dr O Brien, thought that one day she would be a vet.   Eileen eventually proved them   wrong. Whilst she had a particular love for animals, she also had a great desire to learn about medicine and bring improvements to the health of the people around her. She secretly sent her application, to, Trinity hospital in Dublin. She eagerly and excitedly waited for the postman to arrive. The days turned to weeks before the letter came

"Jaysus Eileen, you expecting the news to say that you have won a fortune"?

"Mammy you won't believe me if I tell you. I've been keeping a secret. I'm waiting for a letter from Dublin. I've applied to medical school. I want to be a doctor."

I felt a surge of pride run through my body. My daughter with ambition. I, within myself, for my own selfish reasons, didn't want Eileen to leave the homestead, and go to Dublin, but for my daughter, I wanted whatever she wanted for herself. I prayed daily that her application would be successful. The day arrived, when the postman rode his bicycle up to our house.

"Jaysus it's a grand day" he muttered, as he handed me a letter with a Dublin postmark. For god's sake, it was winter time, it was cold and rainy so how could he possibly think that it was a grand day? I called Eileen down from the top field. She looked happy, but very nervous at the same time.

" Give it to me Mammy, give me the letter"

After what seemed like an eternity, but was probably half an hour or so, of deliberation, she slowly peeled the envelope open, and pulled out the piece of paper. She took more time, before eventually reading the result. The disappointment for her was huge, when at the age of 21; she failed her 1st year entrance exam to medical school.   Eileen, who would usually appear to be so untouched by everything, was now visibly distressed by the news. She cried, firstly in silence, but then in rage.

"Come on Eileen, get it out of your system"

I squeezed my daughter till I couldn't squeeze her any more. She wiped the tears from her face. She read the letter again. Would she get support from her younger sister I wondered? I did hope so. It's a time like this, that sisters need each other, and can be such an immense comfort, when nothing else seems fair.

" Look Eileen, here's Kathy now. She's coming down the borreen. You need to tell her what's happened. Tell her that your application didn't succeed and you won't be leaving us after all."

Kathy was shocked by her own reaction to Eileen's failure. All of a sudden she realised that although she didn't want Eileen to leave, she was sad for her when she failed her exams. She was almost shocked, to see Eileen having to wipe the tears from her face.

"Eileen you're the strong one you can't be like this".

She hugged her sister, like she was going to squeeze the life out of her

"You have to work for another year, work hard, don't worry about the family. I will help mammy on the land, you go off and be with Dr O Brien. That's where you will get some knowledge, and some experience. The knowledge that you will need to successfully complete one of those damn things. Why didn't they just take you Eileen? We know you have the brains to do it. Pity they couldn't see that."

Kathy found herself getting angry! Writing answers to bloody questions on a bloody piece of paper is not a true assessment of a person's ability.

" You will try again, and I know you will succeed, you will Eileen, do you hear me?"

Kathy was confused by her own mixed feelings. She knew that she was growing up. This was a mature way to think, and put your own selfish feelings to one side. Kathy felt proud of herself. She did offer Eileen support and compassion, in a way that I didn't think she could have done. She offered her reassurance about the land, and about caring for the family. Kathy made me proud. She loved her sister. She has just demonstrated this, and would now try to continue, to put Eileen's needs before her own feelings. Kathy realised that being selfish is not a good trait in anyone and she wouldn't be that person any longer

Eileen truly appreciated the comfort shown by her sister. She told Kathy how much it meant to her, to have her sisters support. To know that she would help look after everything in Eileen's absence. Eileen was, as ever, very focused. She was a little annoyed with herself. She too, couldn't quite understand why she had failed, in her words,

"This bloody paper".

Maybe, she had been having a bad day when she filled it in? Maybe her thoughts had been with her boyfriend and not on the job at hand. She had a great determination to be successful the next time round. She studied hard for the following year. She did voluntary work on the wards at Castlebar. Helping Matron was her favourite activity. Matron was very knowledgeable. She too had wanted to be a doctor however family life got in the way of her studies. Matron admired Eileen's determination and offered encouragement together with information that would hopefully be beneficial to Eileen on her next application to Medical School. The journey to Castlebar was a tedious one. Eileen was fit and healthy. She cycled the thirty two miles to the hospital and home again the same day one day per week for the following year. Eileen also spent many hours with Dr O Brien, shadowing him in his surgery, accompanying him on home visits, and endlessly borrowing books which he recommended for her.

Padraig was never certain, of his own feelings and thoughts, around the whole situation. Did he really want Eileen to leave for Dublin? Padraig had a very jealous type of nature. He remembered what happened, when a first cousin of his went away to study, leaving the boyfriend at home, and her meeting someone else who was on the same academic level as she was. Padraig couldn't bear the thought of this happening to him. He decided that he had to do something. He must stop Eileen from leaving, to study, to become a doctor. He wouldn't be able to cope, with the idea of his girl friend being smarter than he was.

"Jaysus Eileen, you're going to get headaches from all that reading. Can't you put the books away for a while?"

Padraig considered proposing to Eileen in the hope that this would keep her at home, however, deep down he was aware that she would probably See through it, and lose all respect for him. He didn't want to be the cause of her, having feelings of resentment for him. After some deliberation, he changed his mind, and decided, that he would try his hardest, to accept, that she has the rights to a career of her choice, and place some trust in the fact, that she says, she loves him and only him. Padraig had made the realisation, that if he tried to keep Eileen for himself, through false ways then they had nothing really. Eileen was beginning to doubt Padraigs intentions. Was he seriously worried for her well being or was he simply having feelings of jealousy? She would never give in to his attempts at manipulation. She decided to talk it through with him, to put him at ease, to reassure him.

"Come over here Padraig come and sit down with me"

Eileen was serious in her tone. Padraig knew, this was going to be, what he could only describe as a session of some description, that would be putting him in his place .He didn't want this, he didn't want to be lectured at by his girlfriend. He had to find an escape route, find a way to avoid this discussion. He had a frown on his forehead that told Eileen, who knew him so well, that he was worried.

"Jesus Mary and Joseph Eileen, I haven't got time for this, the cows have to be brought in for milking"

Eileen extended her arm in his direction, taking hold of his hand. Eileen has great intuition and knew exactly how Padraig was feeling. She knew that the power of reassurance lay within her; she simply had to convince her boyfriend

"Its all right Padraig, you don't need to be worried. I simply wish to help you believe that I want only you"

The discussion went well. Eileen has the magical touch needed, to reassure, when reassurance is required. Padraig gave her a hug before he went off to get the cows.

Eileen accompanied Dr O Brien when he had to pronounce one of the villagers, (Johnnie O Docherty) as being dead. Johnnie had lived in the next village to Eileen's family all of his life. He was a dear old man now aged Ninety four years. Eileen had spent many a day watching him on his farm, and sometimes, helping make the hayricks with him. Johnnies wife, together with his family were at his bedside reciting the rosary and sprinkling holy water from Knock Shrine round the room. Eileen could smell the faintest hint of incense; the priest had just left the house, and left his mark behind him. Johnnies wife, looked like she could be joining Johnnie, anytime soon. Poor old thing sitting crouched in the corner, with hardly a bit of meat on her bones. With a tear rolling down her face, and a voice that was full of quivers, she shook Eileen's hand, and wished her well in her career. Eileen struggled with her own emotions. This was hard for her. She thought she was going to faint. She had only ever seen one person dead. All the memories came flooding back. Her dear, dear father, laying there in his hospital bed, he had looked so white, the blood drained from his body and now she had to see it all again. Her mind wandered, but was quickly brought back to focus.

"You want to be a doctor Eileen O Hara, you better get used to looking at the corpse"

Dr O Brien was a little sharp in his tone. He was willing Eileen to pass her resits, and hurry up and relieve him, from the position that he is now struggling to keep up with. The journey from his home, to his surgery, is almost too much for him, and that's before he saddles up the horse to go and do the school immunisations or whatever else his day demands from him. He also wished to have some time for leisure, maybe take a trip to the States, to catch up with family who had immigrated there many years ago, before the day comes for him to meet his maker. Eileen composed herself, and decided that Dr O Brien had the right attitude. She would detach her emotions, when in the work place, that way, hopefully, she would make a better doctor.

At last, the letter arrived. Eileen had got her appointment through. Three more weeks, and then she would go to Dublin to do it all over again. The day arrived. Eileen was up before dawn. She paced the house a few times then took a brisk walk down to the river. Her stomach was churning. Eileen couldn't believe how nervous she was feeling. She knew how to release her anxieties. Walking was her way. She did four trips, fetching buckets of water from the spring well each time. Eventually after a cup of hot tea and some fresh soda bread, she was on her way to Dublin. Eileen had already done a half days work, before catching the eleven o'clock train. She arrived at the hospital feeling good ,feeling inspired by the Matron from Castlebar and by Dr O Brien . Eileen was shown into the examination area for new students. She sat at her desk took some deep breaths and opened the envelope which contained the resit papers. The questions seemed real easy. She had a reasonable air of confidence about her. She could remember well from the text books given to her by Dr O Brien. Eileen did her resits. She went back home that day, with the decision, that if she failed this time, she would give up her desire to be a doctor and probably train in nursing. After all she could maybe get a job like the Matron in Castlebar. Two months later she received her response from the examination section of the Hospital. The letter came with the Dublin postmark. Eileen was over in Castlebar helping out on the wards. I left the letter on the dresser, until she got home, and had a rest before opening it.

" Oh mammy will you open it for me"

Eileen was out of character in this request. I decided not to help her out. I knew that she would regret her weakness later.

"Be Jaysus Eileen will you just open the thing"

She did, and her dream began. She had been accepted at Trinity hospital in Dublin to study to be a doctor. It was all there. All the details of when she should arrive, who she should report to, and all of that. Eileen was very modest about her achievement very excited at the same time. She agreed that we could have a small get together in her honour. I didn't do things in a small way

Eileen should have known that. We arranged a celebration party, well a few glasses of port, and a Guinness, or two, with a tray of woodbines(Cigarettes) being passed round. Everybody, including Padraig, was happy for Eileen, and the fact, that at last she could pursue her dreams.

Kathy didn't have those ambitions, those dreams. She was much more laid back than her sister. She was happy milking the cows and feeding the pigs, with a very keen interest in one of the sons of the McGeever family, who lived two villages away from ours.

"Mammy he's a nice lad and he loves the farm. Sure there's no harm in going to the dance with him now is there?"

Kathy went into deep thought. Her mind was wandering, wondering about Michael. She remembered that he had told her, that he can feel music vibrating through the floor boards. He watches people and follows their moves.

"Oh mammy, have I told you that Michaels deaf. Life's not fair is it?"

Kathy had a look of despair on her face then quickly changed to a smiling face "But Michael doesn't let it stop him, so I'm not going to let it get me down either".

I wondered about his brothers and sisters. Did they have the same disability? Kathy was angry with me!

How could I suggest that her boyfriend is disabled? He didn't have that acceptance, and it's that attitude that has got him through. Michael had meningitis as a very young child. He lost his hearing but is lucky that he doesn't have brain damage or even have lost his life. I had never heard of meningitis. Kathy explained very well what a horrible illness it is. I thought about how hard it must be for Kathy having a friend who couldn't speak. I admired her, for her broad mindedness.

"Sure Kathy there's a lot who would ignore poor Michael".

She didn't appreciate those comments. I didn't often see Kathy angry, but now she was.

"Mammy for Christ's sake, why is he poor Michael? Yes he might be deaf, but in many ways he has a better life than I do ".

She stormed out of the house and stayed out for the rest of the day. The weather wasn't the best. Kathy didn't take a coat. I did worry a little, because I had upset her, and that was never my intention. I imagined that she had gone to Michael's . Later that evening, Eileen told me, that she had seen Kathy going down the borreen to the McGeevers house. I felt relieved. It was a good feeling to know that she had an escape from me, another person that she could go to, when things got a little difficult between us. Kathy spent many hours at the McGeevers. Michael was a couple of years older than her.

"Michael likes me. He likes me being there to make cups of tea, and help bake the soda bread. I've being spending time with his family, learning how to do the deaf speech. Its brilliant mammy, you use your hands instead of your mouth. I can talk to Michael about anything now, and he said that maybe one day, I might like to teach this in the school".

There are so many different signs to be used, and to be used with great caution, as it would be very easy to give the wrong message. Kathy was unusually immersed in deep thought

Me, working in a school teaching, Oh I don't know about that. Think that I'm more suited to milking the cows, but Michael's right; everyone should learn how to speak to deaf people, and learn that being deaf means just that, it doesn't mean that you're stupid. People have proven themselves to be very ignorant. Ignoring Michael's attempts to communicate with them. He has learned to switch his voice off. That's less intimidating to the ignorant, as a deaf person can make quite harsh sounds when they try to communicate.

"Jaysus mammy what do you think? Do you think that I should try to do it? You know me well.Do you think that I'm smart enough? I'm not like Eileen you know with all her brains".

I told my daughter that she can do anything that she puts her mind to, and the choice is going to have to be hers, but yes I do think she should do it.

"Michael's mammy said that you have taught me well. That I make the best soda bread she's ever tasted and isn't that just great that I can make a dying woman happy, and it's all thanks to you mammy".

I was surprised at this statement, I had no idea Michael's mammy was ill, let alone dying. Kathy seemed upset. She had a quiver in her voice

." Michael's mammy is sick. She's going to die, she has cancer of the liver and there's no cure. She has already been to the hospital in Dublin, on four occasions. They said that she has about six months left".

Kathy became very emotional, the tears quietly rolling down her face. I held her close

"Shhh there Kathy".

She began to sob uncontrollably. I tried to reassure her.

" Oh Kathy there must be a way, there has to be a way. I know what we will do; we will go to Knock. We will go to the holy shrine of our Lady, and pray for Michael's mammy, and we will do it soon. I will go tomorrow to get the bus tickets. Michael can come too and say some special prayers. He can bring her holy water to sprinkle in her room, and to bless herself with. Would you like that Kathy?"

Kathy nodded. The decision is made then, so that's what we will do. Kathy wondered to herself about how much she knew her own mammy. She was surprised by the amount of interest shown from her mammy, in the future prospects of the McGeever family, and in particular Mrs Mc Geever. Kathy felt a sense of warmth within her soul. She thanked God for the good caring family she comes from

Two days later we all left for Knock. We had to be up very early. The bus left at 8am. Barney was saddled up and ready to go at 6.30. Padraig had got up early too; he took us to the bus in Ballagh. We arrived in Knock at 10am. Kathy or Michael had never been this far out of their own small rural villages. They were amazed at the beauty of it all. We had a look around the shops. Mostly displaying the rosary beads, and prayer and picture cards of St Martin and St Patrick. There was the odd statue of the Virgin Mary selling for sixpence. I couldn't really afford to buy anything but realised how precious a statue would seem to Michael's mammy. My thoughts were focused on the future. We will have some money from the pig market next month; surely I can spare a few shillings. We had lunch in a very tiny bar near the Shrine. Michael continued to be anxious to get to the chapel. I hoped that his expectations wouldn't be too high, that he wouldn't be too disappointed. I wasn't quite sure what he was expecting from this trip. The sense of peace within the old chapel, in some sort of strange way, was comforting and reassuring. We all prayed, and lit candles for our loved ones who had gone before us. I spent special time, with my thoughts focused on John, and wondering what he would make of all this here at knock. Michael spent nearly two hours on his knees praying. He probably thought that if he prayed to every Saint that he could think of, it would increase the prospects of a cure for his mammy. Poor Michael, he almost looked helpless as he knelt in front of the Shrine.

"Come on Michael it's getting late, we need to be going before we miss the bus".

The journey home was tense and tiring. The bus weaved its way through all the sleepy lanes. Kathy fell asleep on Michaels shoulder. Padraig met us in Balla with Barney and the cart. It was good to get home, have a cup of tea, and a slice of soda bread, with homemade butter. Michael walked from our house back home. He said that he wanted the exercise, before getting back and having to face the pain on his mammy's face again. I'm not sure how he was feeling but imagine that it was pretty rough. Kathy had shown me a few signs, so I was able to tell Michael that we would be there to support him. I was shocked when he opened his arms and hugged me.

"Thank you Mrs O Hara"

Michael had used his voice; I could just about make out the words. I felt humbled; that a young man with his difficulties had made such a fervent attempt to communicate with me. The stress was beginning to show on Kathy. She was lethargic and restless during the day time. She seemed to have lost her zest for life.

Sleeping had become a problem for her, with some nights, only managing to sneak four or five hours, and other nights, almost nothing at all. What was happening she wondered? Irritation was beginning to replace the calm serenity that usually was part of her persona. She lost her resolve to be supportive of her sister. Kathy could now only think about herself. Because of this, she was disappointed in herself. The determination she once had, now seemed to be flowing out of her body. She had been unable to maintain her willingness to put her sister before herself and because of this she was having feelings of self shame. I can still hear her protests ringing in my ears, when Eileen, at the age of twenty two, calmly gave us the news, that, the letter of confirmation had arrived; she would be off to Dublin for six years to study medicine. At last she was going to realise her dreams.

" You can't Eileen, you can't leave mammy and me, what about me, who will I complain too when everything is going wrong ?.

 And everything is going wrong right now. Michael's mammy is dying and I cannot cope. I cannot cope seeing Michael so upset all the time, and now you're leaving too.Jaysus Eileen, how I wish that daddy was here. You wouldn't go then, he wouldn't let you go. He would make you change your mind, he would". Kathy was beside herself. She wiped her tears. Oh god Eileen I will miss you. Kathy was relentless in her outburst. Whenever Eileen attempted to interject and respond, Kathy would talk over her with further anxieties

"What about Padraig , what will he say? Have you told him yet, well have you?

She was demanding answers from her sister in the same way that she did when they were little girls. Eileen eventually managed to respond and tried to give some reassurance. She hugged her sister. A big warm embrace that was soothing and comforting and above all reassuring.

" It's not for ever, Eileen whispered in her ear. The time will go very quick, and there will be many rewards, not just for me, but for you also, and for the community in general"

Kathy calmed herself down. She wiped her tears away. She stopped shouting and listened to Eileen. She knew her sister very well. She knew that Eileen's mind was made up, she wanted to practise medicine and that was that. Nothing and no one was going to stop her, and sure, it would only be six years and what's that out of a lifetime.   Eileen hugged her sister again.

" I will miss you too Kathy. I will miss mammy and Padraig and this place. Even the stink coming from the pig house, but I do have to go. It's what I want to do, and remember, that when daddy died, we all said that medicine is not advanced enough. That it needs new blood, young fresh blood with new ideas and a passion to make advance in all areas of medicine. To find better ways of helping the sick, find cures for disease, and to take part in protests about the distance to the nearest hospital. Jaysus Kathy look how far it is for Michael's mammy when she needs treatment. How uncomfortable daddy was, on the long journey to Castlebar. I have that passion for medicine Kathy. It burns within me like a roaring fire that will never be put out. I can help to improve things. Maybe I can start a group to raise money to build another hospital, a good hospital with the finest doctors that Ireland has ever seen. We can try to coax them from America. Everyone says that America leads the world in medicine. Maybe a few handsome ones at that, as well as being good doctors".

The girls giggled for a few minutes.

" We won't tell Padraig or Michael... Jaysus no, we can't have them getting jealous now can we".

The girls giggled some more. Suddenly Eileen became very serious again.

" You will be proud Kathy when you see my name up there. Eileen O Hara, fundraiser extraordinaire Oh and American doctor seducer".

The girls were laughing again, at the sheer thought of the idea, but then, Kathy realised that Eileen had never been more serious about anything in her whole life. Kathy focused her own thoughts once more. She remembered how good she had felt about herself when she was supporting Eileen. She excused herself for how she is now by reminding herself of Michael's situation, and then, quite suddenly, she can see flashes in her mind. Flashes of how, maybe, Eileen could help to change medicine, and improve the life's of others, and maybe even get some help for the next person who develops the same problem as Michaels mammy. Eileen too is deep in thought

"Maybe I could do those things Kathy. You wouldn't want to deny me those opportunities now would you? You wouldn't want to deny anyone a better quality of life. I know you wouldn't, your just a bit panicky right now .Jesus Mary and Joseph who wouldn't be in your situation?"

The girls hugged each other. Eileen knew that it would be all right, that Kathy would be all right. Eileen had been trying to find ways, to help her sister see that going off to Dublin for six years studying medicine could be a great thing to do, with the possibility of many positive outcomes for the community. She now knew that Kathy would understand and be the mature young woman she could be. To say that the following four weeks were hectic for Eileen would be an understatement. People to see, things to do, goodbyes to be said. The girls worked very hard, and very much together, in order to ensure that Eileen, was fully prepared, for the new adventure she was about to embark upon. Those weeks saw lots of laughter, and lots of tears, between them.

Eileen Leaves For Dublin

At last, the day of leaving arrived. There was a degree of tension in the house. The lantern had blown out. The night's storm was awfull. I could hear the rain pelting down. The wind had blown over a piece of old wood, that John had put up, against the back window. It was in the run, between the pig house and the house we lived in. John had put the wood on a sloping angle

"Well Biddy the pigs do need exercise you know"

John had some strange ideas. He thought that he could teach the pigs to run up and down the wooden plank. I prayed that the storm would calm down before we left. It was a Sunday, and we had to forget about mass. I suddenly realised that Eileen hadn't been to confession for about four weeks. Her mind had been so occupied, with what she was embarking upon that she forgot her commitments to the lord.

"Be Jaysus Eileen, I'm sure in the circumstances that God would have forgiven us".

Would the judgemental neighbours though? There have been occasions when the children were growing up, that you couldn't always make the eleven O Clock. The childless couple, living across the other side of the borreen, in the thatched house with just one window, and a dirty one at that, somehow always managed to know just what everyone else was getting up to. They had mundane life's I suppose, and had to find a way to pass the time, and create some level of interest for themselves. I often said a prayer for them, that God might give them some understanding of family life. That he might help them, to be supportive, to the less fortunate than themselves. We do believe that some prayers go unheard, those must be the ones, because that couple, openly criticise, every mistake we make, every time we make one, and there's plenty of them.

Kathy was up bright and early. Everyone knew how she was feeling about her sister leaving, naturally I was anxious about how she would behave, but underneath that anxiety, I knew my daughter well, and had a quiet confidence that it would be all right. That she would put her sister first. Kathy came into the seated area, holding a cup of tea.

"Come over here Eileen, get this down you"

She placed the tea next to her sister, and then came outside to where I was milking a cow. Kathy had clearly made her mind up. She was going to be brave.

"I won't let her down mammy. I won't allow my sister to go away to Dublin, having to worry about anything, or anyone that she's leaving behind."

53

She would fight back the tears till Eileen had gone. Kathy decided that this had to be hard for her sister too. She would show her support.

"Don't worry about a thing Eileen, I will look after mammy and the cows, and keep an eye on Padraig too "

"Not too close an eye I hope".

Eileen joked with her sister as they collected the last few things to go to Dublin.

Eileen O Hara, behave yourself. The girls giggled to each other, as they wandered outside to see where Padraig was. He was in the top barn. Kathy heard him crying. She felt surprised. She didn't realise that Padraig had such a degree of sensitivity. She had to distract Eileen, she couldn't allow her to see, just how upset her boyfriend was. She told her to go back in the house. Make another cup of tea for everyone.

"Oh Jaysus Padraig, pull yourself together"

She pulled out a rather grubby looking handkerchief from her pocket. She offered it to Padraig. Eileen can't see you like this it will break her heart. He wasn't sure. He wasn't convinced, despite her many efforts to reassure him, that his girl friend cared all that much for him. Kathy hugged him, then whispered in his ear

"I know her; I know she wants you, as well as wanting to be a doctor. She can do both you know Padraig. She can have her career, and have you, the love of her life at the same time".

He decided that he would listen to Kathy, that he would believe what she was telling him. This way, the parting, the saying goodbyes, would be nicer. He decided that he had to lose his insecurities before it cost him the loss of Eileen. Jaysus, at last, he was seeing sense.

"Your all right you know Kathy, you have a sensible head".

Padraig pulled her close and hugged her. He got his coat and went outside to see what needed to be done. He loaded the cart. We all set out for the ten o clock in the morning train. The day was windy and bleak looking. We huddled together, in the open cart, keeping each other warm. Padraig had the reins

"Gee up Barney"

A gentle tap to Barney's side made him trot a little faster. Kathy had made up a bottle of tea, and buttered eight slices of Eileen's favourite currant brack. She could be such a thoughtful girl. We stopped the horse and cart just outside Ballagh. We had a second breakfast. The tea was still warm but only just. Eileen was very excited but a little anxious at the same time. She was wondering how Kathy was really feeling and how she is going to cope without her sister.

"The time will fly by Kathy"

You make sure that you bake some bread for Michael's mammy, and I will make sure, that I try to find the best doctor in Dublin hospital, and talk to him, or her, about the care of cancer patients. That will be my first job when I get there and that's a promise. You can tell that to Michael. Tell him that I will be looking out for the best, and sending them to see his mammy. Kathy had a look of relief on her face. She knew her sister wouldn't let her down and that if there was any hope for Michael's mammy then Eileen would find it.

The train, was twenty five minutes late arriving at the station, and then, after every single last person had climbed on board, it sat there for another twenty minutes or so. Tension was mounting. The wait felt like an absolute eternity. Eileen was leaving, so we all wished to get it over with. It was winter time, so not easy to keep warm. Eileen was wearing her thick, black and grey, tweed coat and a pair of real leather ankle boots, to keep the rain and any snow out. We knew that she would be warm enough in Dublin. As the train pulled away from the station, we wiped the tears that we had worked so hard at holding inside ourselves, till she had gone. The windows on the train were steamy, and not the cleanest either. Eileen had sat in an empty cubicle, but then she was joined by two other young women. They all seemed to be chatting away to each other. There was a big black belt holding the seat down, it was like the big black cloud in my heart. My daughter had left for medical school. I should be happy.

I was happy in some ways, but obviously, as her mother, I did have some concerns. Would she be lonely? Has she made the right decision? Would she look after herself properly? Would she go to confession and receive Holy Communion every Sunday morning? The thoughts, the worries were endless, but I couldn't express them. Isn't that just how it is for a mother? Trying to keep the best side out, for the sake of everyone else.

Padraig had held Eileen so tightly I thought she would burst. The look on his face as the train pulled away was one of pain that I knew I wouldn't forget for a long time .Kathy had been braver than I ever imagined she could possibly be, but now my shoulders were drenched. And what about me? I kept my thoughts to myself. Trying to be positive for the sake of everyone else, never showing any emotion, but secretly worrying for both of my girls. Although Eileen was the one who had ventured away, she was the stronger one, so Kathy had most of my concern. I was trying to figure out in my mind, some plans to keep her busy. Maybe some painting jobs or something like that. The home journey was much faster. Barney trotted away without too much encouragement. It was a lighter load for him to pull. Be Jaysus you would think that Eileen was off for a lifetime, with the amount of stuff she crammed into that case. We arrived back home, just in time, to get the praties, cabbage and boiled bacon on the go. Everyone was very hungry, so it was clean plates all round. Padraig enjoyed his meal with us. He returned back to his own home, just in time for the evening rosary. Kathy seemed a little down. She wondered, about exactly what her sister might be doing, at that very moment. The house seemed quiet. It was only one person down, but felt more than that. Dr O Brien dropped by that evening. He had wondered how the whole day had gone. We lit the lanterns early, had some supper, said our prayers and went to bed. It seemed like the best thing to do.

"If you close your mind Kathy, you won't miss her till the morning".

Kathy usually appreciated my advice, usually thinking, that mammy always knows best in those matters. This time she wasn't too sure. That first week was a very long one. At last the weekend arrived. We were all excited. Then the telegram came. Eileen had got a bad dose of the Asian flu. She wouldn't be coming home for a while.

" Mammy I'm so sorry. I should be ok for next weekend though".

She wasn't. We had never before been separated from my daughter for this long. Kathy was amazing. She was reassuring Padraig almost on a daily basis. Three weeks later was Eileen's first visit back to her home place. Padraig saddled the horse up. We arrived in Ballaghaderreen forty minutes before the train was actually due in. Coffee in Mulligan's was on order.Padraig thought that maybe he would have a stout whilst he waited. At least he listened to my advice that Eileen would not be overly happy, to be greeted by him, sniffing of alcohol. When the train pulled in, we were all jumping with excitement. Despite everything she looked quite well .Padraig took her case, then he held her for what seemed like ever more. There was so much to talk about. Poor Eileen, so many questions from all of us. Padraig was unusually quiet. It felt, as though he simply wished to look at her in silence. Like he couldn't believe that she had come back. Couldn't believe that she still wanted him in her life. A few neighbours came over that night. One man brought his flute and some woodbines. Despite being under the weather as a result of the flu, Eileen still enjoyed herself and did a few steps of the hornpipe before retiring for the night. The weekend went so fast. Before we knew it the time had arrived for her to leave again. Eileen decided that she would live in Dublin, for long periods at a time, coming home only for the weekends. Every six weeks, saw all of us, back at that train station, waving goodbye to her ,as she would once again, reassure everyone, and especially Kathy and Padraig, that time flies by when you keep busy.

Eileen had set up a project for Kathy, to give her a focus, so she didn't spend her time moping about missing her older sister. Hand embroidery held an interest for her. The teacher always said that Kathy had talent when she used her hands. She would spend hours as a small child making handkerchiefs to give away as Christmas presents. I can send them to Santa

Claus, and then he can bring them to children on Christmas morning. The girls used to long to know what Santa Claus looked like and to try to understand the mystery of the whole Santa's coming thing. John would tell them

"On your knees say three hundred hail Marys, one glory be to the father and one our father, every night during the season of advent. If you don't then Santa won't come!"

I suppose that this had been one way of buying a couple of hour's peace and quiet before bedtime. During that time of the year, the girls had been the most obedient they ever were. Eileen told her sister about some jobs that needed doing over at the O Shaunesseys.

"Kathy the bottom room in Padraigs house needs some curtains, something cheerful and bright. Mrs O Shaunessey suffers from bad headaches. She would benefit from something heavy weight to keep the light out. Maybe you could get some material from Flanagan's and surprise them".

Flanagan's was the local drapers, on Main Street in Balla, not too expensive either. The shop had been there through the generations. " Mammy will take you next time she goes to the town, here's three shillings, spend it carefully". Eileen was very generous. She really didn't have many shillings and could have used them for herself in Dublin. Typical of her she put others before herself. Eileen didn't believe her own story about the family needing new curtains, so she wondered how convincing it would be, to her sister. Kathy actually didn't believe it either, however, she played the game, and to her amazement enjoyed doing so .She thought about the money, and reached the conclusion that if Eileen gave it to her, then that's what Eileen wanted to do, so now everybody would be happy. Three shillings, was just one penny more than she needed for the material that Flanagan's had put in their sale, and it was enough to buy fabric for two pairs of curtains. It was Kathy's lucky day. Annette O Shaunessey was a very proud woman, so Kathy wondered how she would feel about her making the curtains. She shouldn't have worried. Annette was very reassuring and to be honest, I don't think that the poor woman would be too bothered anyway. She did have more serious things to think about, such as her own failing health. She was a strong woman, but the strongest of people would surely know if their body was playing host to the dreaded cancer. Her secret was a very well kept one, well for the time being anyhow. There was nothing to see, so people would never guess, well not for now anyhow. Annette had thought to herself that she wouldn't tell her family until she absolutely needed to. Cancer, if that's what it is, that's wrong with Mrs Shaunessey, would surely take her life, but until she had that confirmation, she would be keeping her mouth shut. She did consider telling Eileen, in secret, in the hope that Eileen would be able to get her some help from this posh hospital that she was going off too. Her response to Kathy's suggestion of new curtains was one of gratitude

"Sure that's grand of you Kathy. That room surely does need brightening up. A pair of heavy weight curtains would be great. Red roses are my favourite flowers, and reds my favourite colour. Will I help you Kathy, or do you enjoy sewing?"

Wont Padraig be pleased when he sees the new look to the window! Kathy smiled to herself. She seemed to remember, seeing material of that description, in the window of Flanagan's shop. She hoped that there would be enough fabric for two pairs of curtains. She would go to town with her mammy, to get everything she needed to get started. Kathy sensed that Padraigs mammy seemed anxious about something."

You all right Mrs Shaunessey".

"Yes darlin I'm all right"

Annette's voice was a little weary. Kathy wasn't convinced. She decided to let Mrs Shaunessey help with the sewing. It might present an opportunity for her to speak about whatever was bothering her. The plan was coming into place. Kathy was excited about her project." I can start on Tuesday week if that's all right with yourself?"

Mrs O Shaunessey seemed to be almost as excited as Kathy was. The ladies sat together in the back room sewing away. A little robin perched on the window ledge. The sunshine showed up all the marks on the glass. It was a fair old time since Mrs Shaunessey had had the energy to be bothered with the cleaning of windows.

"You all right Mrs Shaunessey ? you don't seem too chirpy today".

Kathy didn't raise her glance. She knew that it would be easier to share things whilst focusing on the sewing."Oh I'm grand darling". There was a change in Annette's voice. A sort of a strain that would only indicate a worry, or something along those lines. Kathy knew something serious was wrong.

"Oh Annette, you should tell me what's wrong. We all need someone to talk to".

Annette broke down. The kindness in Kathy's voice was too much.

"Jaysus what's wrong, what can be that bad "

Annette told Kathy, that she thinks she might have cancer. She has no energy, Very bad moods, gets angry with the family for no reason. Sweats a lot, especially at night time, and sometimes her whole body goes hot from head to toe.

" No Annette. I'm no doctor, but I'm pretty sure that you don't have cancer. Come over and sit with me for a few minutes. Have you any soda bread or currant brack?"

Kathy looked in the box in the kitchen, found the bread, made the tea and told Annette to eat away whilst she finished the bit of sewing she had started. Kathy was thinking to herself, wondering how she should attempt to tell Annette, that it's more likely that she was on the change of life than anything else being wrong. She remembered her own mammy telling her and Eileen, all about it, when she started the change. Kathy decided that she would use the same approach.

"Annette I know that I'm just a kid, but there's something's that my mammy has shared with me, about life, that I would like to share with you"

Go ahead Kathy tell me what you want to share. Kathy began...."Jaysus this is harder than I thought it would be." She took a deep breath. Ok When women turn a certain age, anything above forty really, their body starts to change. They can feel all of the things, that you told me you feel, and eventually their periods stop so no more making babies. Annette was shocked. No one had told her about this change in a woman's life. She was aged fifty one, and had been feeling like this for several months now. She hadn't had a period for seven months.

"Jesus Mary and Joseph Kathy. This must be what's wrong with me then".

Annette was relieved. She no longer worried about cancer. Kathy continued

"My mammy said that the best way to try to help yourself, to cope with those feelings, is to go for long walks".

Annette made a promise to herself that she would have no more thoughts about cancer, that she would take Kathy's advice, and that the future would be brighter for her, and in turn for her family. Kathy realised, that she had the ability, and the maturity, to be able to help another person. She said goodbye to Annette and returned the following day to finish the curtains.

New Admirers

Eileen loved her time in Dublin. She would often go out in the evenings by herself, for a long walk, and occasionally, she would have a coffee in the bar at the end of O'Connell Street. Eileen was a popular girl. She didn't need to be alone. She was a people's person, with great social skills and a great sense of humour. She had the knack of changing a bad situation into something humorous, but keeping the ambience there at the same time. She had many admirers at the hospital where she was doing her training. Fellow students often attempted to coax her out to the pub in the evenings after work.

"Be Jayuss Eileen, all work, and no play, and all that "

Going to the pub with friends was not Eileen's scene. She wasn't listening, not even when to her amazement, a consultant,(Mr Corcoran) on one of the wards she was delegated to, had shown an interest in her .

"There's a play on, in the city next week Eileen .I've managed to get two tickets. I know you would like it, would you like to join me?"

Eileen had never seen a play. She didn't share that information with Mr Corcoran. She imagined that he would consider her very sheltered, if he knew the environment she had come from. Eileen was flattered by his interest, and said that she needed time to think about it. She was very much in love with Padraig, and would never cheat on him; however, she didn't wish to knock Mr Corcoran back just like that. She didn't wish to offend him. In some ways she didn't really know how to respond. She didn't really know very much about Mr Corcoran. She presumed that as a hospital Consultant, he must be a decent type of person. Possibly a pillar of the community that everyone looked up to. Why was he still single at his age? and with his education, and she presumed integrity! That evening she sat quietly in her room thinking, amongst other things, about the invitation from Mr Corcoran. Wondering to herself, what it is, he could find interesting about her. After all, she's simply a plain girl from the countryside and he's a medical consultant from Kilkenny town. It all seemed a little odd to Eileen that he demonstrated this interest in her. Suddenly, there was a knock at her door

"Time for a cuppa tea and a chat" a fellow student wondered.

"Come in Geraldine, sure it's a cold night to be standing out there".

Eileen organised the tea .Would you care for a bite to eat? There were a few slices of currant brack in the box. They were starting to look like they had seen better day's .The girls enjoyed them, heavily spread with butter. Eileen began day dreaming. Not as good as mammy's butter she thought to herself. Eileen knew that her friend was a townie girl, therefore probably had never experienced the joys of homemade butter from her own kitchen. Eileen felt lucky. There's so many experiences come from living on a farm. She wished that her friend could share those experiences and maybe one day she will do so. Maybe one day she would visit Eileen's homeland and feel the joys of the freedom of the fields. Experience the very different way of life, where your days begin at dawn and don't end till dusk. The girls exchanged some gossip about the new nurse on ward twenty three. Geraldine went off to use the toilet. She many times wondered if she had a weak bladder because one cup of tea and she was almost leaking. There must have been a queue. Eventually after about ten minutes Geraldine returned back to Eileen's room.

"What's the craic then Eileen, her friend asked?"

Eileen wondered if she should tell her about Mr Corcoran. She didn't know Geraldine all that well, therefore she decided not to, as she wasn't too sure of the trust thing.

"Oh nothing much, you know how it is, long days on the wards too tired at the end of it all, to have any excitement, how about yourself?"

"Oh same here, never anyone to have a date with, although of course I could have been on a date with a rat if I had chosen to".

"Jaysus girl, tell me more"

Eileen was keen to hear the gossip. She was thinking, how her own life was so mundane and boring; she had to get her excitement from somewhere.

" You wouldn't believe me Eileen; you will think that I'm making it up".

"No, no, not at all, go on, go on, go on".

Eileen was eager for the information, and didn't wish her friend to shut up now.

"All right then, but you have to promise me not to tell anyone. Geraldine looked a bit coy almost like she had done something wrong when she knew that she hadn't. There was a slight quiver in her voice as she began. There's a consultant on ward forty three. Geraldine needed more reassurance before she could continue. You will keep this secret Eileen, wont you. All right then, a man in his thirties or early forties I would say, so he's done well for himself from an academic point of view. Well, there we were one evening, sitting together when the phone rang. He was busy, so asked me to answer. By the time I had connected with the caller, the consultant had gone to talk to one of his patients. I asked the caller to leave a message. Suddenly Geraldine's face welled up with anger .The bloody

Bastard . It was his wife on the phone wanting to know when was he coming back to Limerick to see his children, and he was the one who had been harassing me to go on a date with him."

There was a look of shock on Eileen's face. She was thinking? Consultant? Limerick? could it be the same one who asked her to go to the theatre?

"Jaysus Geraldine, why did you turn him down for the date although it's a good job that you did"? "Not my type, simple as that, but what a lucky escape I've had".

Eileen decided to ask his name.

" Gerry Corcoran, is his bloody name, and every woman, working in this hospital should know what he's like".

"Jaysus Geraldine I'm tired, would you mind going, and we can meet up another evening, would that be all right".

The girls said goodnight. Eileen felt anger welling up inside of her. She had a conversation with herself. Does Gerry Corcoran think that his position within the hospital, gives him permission to behave in such an awful way? Should she have shared with Geraldine that he was the same man, who wanted to take her to the theatre?

The next shift, on ward forty three, was to say at the least a little difficult. Gerry Corcoran was sitting at the desk when Eileen arrived for her duties. She tried to avoid him. She was walking across the ward when he called after her

"Doctor O hara, can I see you for a minute please".

Eileen took a deep breath "Yes Mr Corcoran"

" Oh Eileen; you don't need to be so formal. He laughed. You can call me Gerry you know. All my friends call me Gerry. Come over, and sit down here beside me. There's coffee in the jug if you want some. I need to share some information with you, about our newest patient who came onto the ward this morning".

Eileen listened attentively, whilst Gerry, went through the medical history, of the lady who came into the hospital last night, then transferred to ward forty three. When he had finished sharing the information, Gerry began to joke with Eileen, about the weather. The noise from the hail stones that were falling, whilst they spoke, was almost as loud, as the noise from the pounding of Gerry's heart, every time he saw Eileen. Despite the fact, that he had asked Geraldine for a date, he was totally infatuated by Eileen. She absorbed his every thought when they were in a room together. Eileen looked uncomfortable. She fumbled for her words.

"Mr Corcoran, Gerry, I need to share some information with you. It's serious and it's very important. Is there somewhere quiet we could go for a few minutes?"

Eileen was feeling very nervous. She felt that, she could put her place at the hospital, in jeopardy, by standing up to Mr Corcoran. However she decided that she had to do it, and take the consequences that might follow. There was another student present who was also attending to the lady in question who had been moved to ward forty three. She was being assessed by Mr Corcoran for her interpersonal skills, as well as her medical ones. He took a few moments to think over Eileen's request and then with a degree of unsteadiness in his voice he exclaimed

"Nurse Brady can you give us a few minutes"

Gerry took Eileen to a small room that was usually reserved for relatives of the seriously sick.

" Jaysus Eileen you look serious. What's this all about?"

"I think you should sit down Gerry. You won't like what I have to say to you.Jaysus Gerry you asked me to go on a date. I was flattered, but would never cheat on Padraig. Padraigs a good man. He loves me. I love him too I will be spending the rest of my life with him. You're a married man, and with children. What are you thinking about? Obviously not about being faithful to your wife, or respecting your children the way a decent father should".

Eileen couldn't believe the way in which she had just spoken to her superior. She almost apologised, but then remembered, that whilst he was a hospital consultant, he was also potentially a cheating

Bastard.The colour drained from Gerry's face. He didn't realise, that she knew he was married.

"Who's told you Eileen? Oh yes, let me guess".

Eileen realised, that Mr Corcoran would have found it hard to take an accurate guess. He realised, that he had asked so many of the students on a date that anyone, of a large number of people, could have told her. Suddenly he felt quite bad, quite ashamed of himself.

"I'm sorry Eileen, you're a nice girl, you deserve better. I shouldn't have tried to involve you in my life. It's just that"

He began to make excuses for his behaviour. Eileen wasn't interested. She had no time for cheats and liars regardless of their reasons.

"Please Eileen, he begged, please hear me out".

Gerry told her about his alcoholic wife who demonstrated more interest in the Guinness bottle, than she had done in him, for years now. Their children were being raised by his sister. In a funny sort of way, Eileen almost felt sorry for him, but put him in his place regarding the potential date.

"Whatever is wrong in your marriage Gerry you have to sort it out? Maybe you should go back to Limerick. Find work in the hospital there. Be close to your wife and children".

Gerry stared out of the window, looking at the raindrops that were falling. He didn't respond to what she had suggested. In fact, he didn't say anything at all, not another word. Eileen wondered why she was bothering. He didn't seem to be interested in what she was saying at all. She decided to return to her patients. I'm going now Gerry I have work to do on the ward. He pulled her back, grabbing her by the arm. He leaned towards her, as if, as if, well she thought he was going to try to kiss her. She slapped his face, then turned, and walked out of the room. The following weeks were a little difficult, a little tense. Eileen constantly wondering if Gerry was going to make trouble for her. Although their paths did cross, the incident was never mentioned again. They maintained a professional working relationship. Eventually she was moved to another department within the hospital. As her superior, Gerry was asked to give a report on the quality of her work. Eileen was astonished. He described her as becoming an excellent doctor with extra skills. He put her name forward, for the prestigious counselling course that was coming up. There were very few places available. All the student doctors were vying for a place. Nine months later, Eileen received a letter in the post. It was from the hospital, requesting the input of all student doctors, to go towards the replacement Consultancy post, for ward forty three. That's when she discovered, that Mr Corcoran had left the hospital. His departure had been simple, and without fuss. He had taken a new look at his life. He had decided, what was really important to him.

"I took the advice of a very wise young woman. She suggested that I should be closer, to my wife and children in the hopes of sorting out my marital difficulties"

Without another word, Gerry shook hands with his superior, said his goodbyes, and left. Eileen was offered a place on the counselling course. She would work towards at the very least a diploma in counselling. She felt better about her discussion with Gerry, realising, that after all, he had listened to her, and appreciated, what she had said. She wrote him a note, wishing him well, and good luck in dealing with his problems. She thanked him for his recommendation for the counselling course. She told him, that on her next visit to Mayo, she would go to the Holy Shrine at knock, where she would pray, for him, and his family, and in particular, for his alcoholic wife, that she would find the strength to give up her addiction. The note was sent on to the hospital that he transferred to, in Limerick. Eileen and Gerry never saw each other, never spoke again. She often wondered how he was. Intuition told her, that he would be doing good, and with his support, so would his wife. Over the years, Eileen had many more invitations to go on dates. Some from married men, some from bachelors. She was never interested. Her one and only love was back in Mayo. Padraig O Shaunessey was a very lucky man. Was my daughter so lucky though?

The Surprise Announcement

It was the evening, after she arrived back from Dublin. The day had been a busy one in the village. Kathy had been fishing in the local river. She caught several trout, and then dug some potatoes. Just enough to make a good meal for us all, including Padraig. Missionaries had been visiting at the chapel. Most people from the local villages had gone to see the Nuns, and brothers, who had come all the way from Africa. Eileen had decided that she wasn't going.

"Jesus Mary and Joseph Eileen, they don't get here very often, surely you can make it"

Those were the words coming from the bottom room. Kathy was in one of her judgemental moods. Everybody should be doing, what she was doing. Kathy's way was the right way, with no room for error of judgement. The Nuns came to our chapel with their mission every two years. The children in particular would get so excited in anticipation of what they might be able to buy from the stalls, set up in the church grounds. It was the usual type of religious artefacts, rosary beads, holy water fonts and pictures of the many saints that we had heard of. Eileen was tired, she had a headache.

" I'm not going Kathy and that's that. I'm sure that the lord will forgive me. I try to do good in my work. I'm sure that I don't need to see the Nuns, to have my path blessed with joy, and contentment, and become deserving of a place in heaven when my time comes".

Kathy was grumbling to herself." Be away with you Eileen" We began our long walk to the chapel, on what was a nice sunny evening. You didn't get too many of them in the West of Ireland. At least it meant that the ground was dry, so we could take the short cut through Dillon's fields. That had to be at least a mile shorter, than walking all the way around the roads. Eileen and Padraig stayed behind in the O Shaunesseys house. They had been left alone in the house.

"You should rest to get rid of that headache"

Eileen was a little surprised, by Padraigs show of concern. He wouldn't usually be that tuned in. Eileen lay on the bed, with a wet cloth on her forehead. The pain was pounding. Padraig made some tea, with lots of sugar, and buttered some soda bread. They ate the bread, and then Padraig went outside for a smoke. By now the weather had changed, the rain was pelting down, onto the thatched roof of the house. He pulled his jacket up over his head, and cursed to himself,

"The Damn weather"

He had twenty woodbines in his pocket. They had been given to him . He had promised himself that when they had gone, then he wouldn't be smoking anymore.

"Be Jaysus Eileen, they're so expensive. No wonder I never have any spare money"

Padraig had decided to try to save his money to buy a small motor car.

"I could drive you back to Dublin"

"But you're always saying that Padraig. You've been saying that for the past two years, and you haven't even started yet. You haven't saved a penny "

"Shh Eileen, you're supposed to be resting, sort your headache out".

Eileen closed her eyes .When she woke, two hours later, she felt better. She went into the small room to sit next to Padraig. He looked tired. She held his hand and kissed him gently on the cheek. They settled in the bottom room for the night. They were in love, and as Eileen would always say where's the wrong in expressing your true feelings, for the person you love, and want to spend the rest of your life with. The following weeks were a little tense for both of them. Eileen realised that she could be pregnant and how that would interfere with her studies. When her period didn't come, she convinced herself, that this happens to young women sometimes, for no particular reason. She felt a little angry with herself, as its one matter, showing your love for someone, it's another matter, taking the possible consequences of that behaviour. Eileen went into deep reflection and felt anger at herself for her lack of responsibility. The second missed period confirmed to her that she would need to give up her studies for some time. Yes, Eileen had got herself pregnant. She was sensible, and hoped that Padraig would be too. She knew that she would eventually, have to stop travelling to Dublin, but for now everything would continue as usual. Eileen had a very liberated attitude and a very open mind. She was aware that Kathy may not share the same openness. She hadn't had the same cultural experiences that Eileen had gained from living in Dublin for the past four year's . On her next weekend home, Eileen asked Kathy if they could go to town together. Kathy was delighted she loved spending time with her sister. The girls went to Donovan's where they enjoyed a coffee and a slice of cake. The craic was good. Eileen decided that the moment for disclosure was right. They were in a public place, so surely, even if Kathy wanted to shout at her sister, she wouldn't.

"Kathy I need to tell you something, I need you to be a friend to me, as well as being my sister, and I need your support possibly more than ever now".

Kathy looked worried. What's wrong Eileen? Are you sick? No. Eileen was pacing herself before she dropped the bombshell.

" I'm pregnant Kathy I'm going to have a baby".

She was disappointed by her sister's reaction. She had expected a little opposition, but not the strength of feeling that Kathy had displayed. Kathy's face was aghast with horror

"Jesus Mary and Joseph Eileen, you can't be pregnant" you can't be, the shame of it all. What will mammy say? What will the neighbours say? You and all your education, your brains, your, your, Oh my God how could you? Have you told Padriag ? What did he say?"

So many questions without any opportunity for Eileen to reply to them. Eileen was shocked by the reaction coming from her sister .How could Kathy be so prudish? How could she not see that her family only cared about the well being of their children, and not the fact that they were being shamed and disgraced, which of course in the eyes of Eileen they weren't. Like I said before, it had to be the four years, of living in the city, the experience of how life is so different there, had opened Eileen's eyes, or, is her sister simply a prude? How could two children born to the same parents be so different in their outlook? Eileen was absolutely going to keep her baby and have it at home, here in this very house and she didn't care how or what people were going to say or react. Eileen had chosen her moment to tell Padraig very carefully. It was a Sunday morning. Everyone had gone to the eleven o'clock mass. Eileen had walked over to the O Shaunessey house early that morning. She asked Padraig to walk over to the river with her.

"Maybe we could catch a trout for tea. Maybe I should race you there "

The two of them set off in the sunshine across the fields. They sat down at the river edge.

"I need to talk to you Padraig it's serious. Our lives are going to change. I'm pregnant. I'm going to have your baby"

The colour drained from Padraigs face. Eileen thought for a minute there that he was going to faint. When he managed to open his mouth for the words to come out, he told Eileen, that he felt very shocked and excited at the same time. He seemed to fully appreciate and understand that Eileen didn't get pregnant all by herself. Padraig was very supportive. He would stand by his responsibilities. Eileen and Padraig were married two months later. The local priest refused to perform the ceremony. His reaction to Eileen and Padraig was hugely lacking in compassion. He had a very angry outburst and didn't give chance for any interruption, until he, had expressed his feelings on the matter. Eileen was thinking to herself that he was not very godly like.

" You're a disgrace to your family Eileen O Hara. Do you have no respect for yourself? And you are studying to be a doctor as well. I would have thought that you would have known better. And as for you padraig O Shaunessey well your just a blegard with no respect for yourself or for god."

Padraigs anger welled up inside him. His fists were clinched together in his pockets. He felt his temperature rising however he knew the difference between right and wrong. He decided to walk away in silence. He didn't trust his own mouth. Eileen was proud of Padraig for his reaction, pleased that he didn't stand and have a shouting match as this was Padraigs usual way of dealing with situations that he didn't like. On this occasion he had demonstrated a sense of respect for the priest. Eileen found it hard to understand how the priest could be this way.

"Father Daniel, Your supposed to represent all things good, to care for, and about people, not to sit in judgement of them "

Eileen was a little distressed but bounced back quickly.

"Your not the only priest around you know. I'm sure another parish will welcome us like I would have expected you too. May god have mercy on you for your ignorance".

Eileen then walked away. There was lots to think about for herself and Padraig. Eileen did reflect on the situation she has found herself in. The determined side of her character came out. She always knew that it would probably be a struggle being an unmarried Mother to be. She would not allow this hiccup with the priest to set her back. Padraig and Eileen went back home. Padraig got on his bicycle and went to Ballaghaderreen. He wanted to check on train tickets for the following day to Sligo where he hoped to visit a priest together with Eileen. The priest agreed to see them. He was an elderly but caring gentleman, who was warm and welcoming. He did not sit in judgement. He possessed a sort of compassion that you wouldn't altogether expect form a religious elderly man. After all Eileen and Padraig in the eyes of the church had committed a serious sin. Sex outside of marriage was and is still strictly forbidden in the Catholic Church. The priest saw the young woman in front of him. He understood about all the opposition she was likely to encounter. He had to be better than all the people who would cast criticism and judgement. He blessed Eileen's unborn child. The marriage took place two months later. It was a small and discreet ceremony. Family only, no friends no neighbours. This was because of financial restrictions and nothing to do with the fact that Eileen was pregnant. An uncle gave her away. Oh how she missed her father, if only he could be there. Eileen wiped her tears

"I know that daddy would be proud to see us getting married. He wouldn't be judgemental about his unborn grandchild "

Eileen wore a plain cream coloured dress. Her slender frame helped to outline the circular shape at the front of her body. This is what Eileen wanted. She was proud. She wanted people to know that she was carrying a child. A love child. An out of wedlock child. Padraig O Shaunesseys child. She loved Padraig and this was a symbol of their love. She did not share the same shameful feelings as her sister. Kathy thought that Eileen should leave the village. In fact, leave Mayo, or even leave Ireland .Kathy, who couldn't really bare to be separated from her older sister, is now so distraught, so ashamed, that she feels that Eileen should move permanently.

" Eileen, you have to go, you can't stay here".

The girls had a furious argument. I don't think that I have ever seen Kathy express such bouts of anger in all her life.

"You gave your body to Padraig. How could you do that, and you were not even married. Now everyone will know that you're a slut Eileen. Kathy's words fell heavy on her sister's ears. Suddenly it seemed like she didn't know her sister anymore. Eileen had expected some resistance but not this. She wondered to herself how Kathy could be so judgemental.

"How dare you try to tell me how to live my life?"

Kathy being Kathy wasn't going to have a change of mind, she continued in her quest to make Eileen feel ashamed, however, it was never going to work!

"Go to Dublin. Go to England even, go anywhere so as not to bring shame on this family. Yourself and Padraig could return to the village in a few years time. You could say that the child is big for its age. The family wouldn't be disgraced".

Kathy thought that she could dictate to her sister. Didn't she know anything? Didn't she know just how strong willed her sister is? Didn't she know that no one tells Eileen how to live her life? Kathy really didn't understand. Eileen was going nowhere. Why should she. She would stay right here in the village. She would hold her head up high, and not be told what to do. She would hopefully have the full support of her family, and that too would include Kathy when she decides to accept the situation. A family, who loved her, loved all their children for what they are, and not for how they behave. Eileen of course was right about the love within our family, however, she didn't seem to understand or think about the fact, that I was from a much older generation, and although I would die for my children, and never let them know my true feelings about anything, the concept of my unmarried daughter getting pregnant, was a hard one for me. I knew that there would be remarks whenever we went to town. I knew that I had to keep my head up high and ignore them.

"Mrs O Hara, sure isn't it your Eileen that's pregnant, we wish her well "

That was the best, I could have hoped for. What usually happened was, as I walked down pound street, in the town, people crossed to the other side, giving me glances, and whispering amongst themselves.

"That's the O Hara woman, away with her; she can't keep her girl under control "

Of course I could understand, to some degree, why they were behaving in this manner. A single, Holy, Catholic, Irish Girl, getting herself pregnant, wasn't acceptable, especially to the older generation. This was my girl though, and that's what made the difference for me. Eileen told them, at the hospital, that she was going to have a baby. Well if she hadn't told them, they would very soon know. Her tummy was getting a little larger and, colleagues had wondered, why she had got married so suddenly. Close friends at the hospital already knew the answer, also knew and understood why the wedding had been so small. Eileen continued with her studies in Dublin, for a further four months. She had an agreement that she would return back to Dublin when her baby reached its first birthday. Eileen accompanied Dr O Brien on his duties, whenever she felt able to, right up to a week before she gave birth.

The Arrival of Martin

At last, the day that they were all waiting for arrived. Eileen felt some twinges in her back. In the beginning she wasn't sure. She hadn't quiet known what to expect. She had during her training in Dublin seen the odd women in labour but had chosen not to get involved. She went for a short walk in the meadow. She called Kathy to get Padraig and to help her round up a few cows thinking the distraction might be good. Then suddenly a gush of water

"Jaysus Padraig it hurts".

Eileen was walking in a stoop. It was too painful to try to stand up straight. She went inside. She paced up and down the house, in, and out, to the meadow for several hours. She drank hot sweet tea, and ate slices of brack and soda bread, with her favourite butter spread thickly. She became a little annoyed and irritated. She was never one for fuss and drama no matter what the situation.

"Stop fussing Padraig, I know my own body, and I know that keeping active is the best thing to do"

Eventually, she agreed that the time was right, for Padraig to send for the midwife, and wasn't that a performance. A neighbour saddled his horse, and then rode the five miles to her house, with the hope that she would be at home, and be available. Three hours later, Mrs Geary, an elderly lady with long greying hair, tied up in a bun, and a brusk attitude arrived on her bicycle. Bicycles or the horse being the usual transport around this way. Motorcars were few and far between. Mrs Geary was tired and a little weary. She had seen better days. She called out to Eileen

"I need some water and a rest before we begin"

She had been the midwife for this village for the past forty years or so, therefore she had attended to the birth of Eileen, and now, here she is again, but this time for Eileen's baby. Eileen was lying down. She was fairly worn out, well truthfully, she was about exhausted and it didn't seem like anything much was going to happen very quickly. Mrs Geary finished her drink of water and decided to go and say hello to her patient.

"Well will you look at you, Eileen O Hara. Oh sure its Eilleen O Shaunessey now and I remember so well the day you popped into this world"

Eileen had been in more sociable moods. She was wishing to herself that the midwife might close her mouth and do an investigation of what was happening. Suddenly it looked as though the whole procedure might not take too much longer. Clean towels and boiled water were the instructions coming from the bottom room intermingled with the cries of

"Oh God help me"

Fortunately padraig had been to the well. Plumbing wise we were still living in the past so the well was the only means of clean water. Towels had been washed in the river and then finished off at home with boiled water, collected from the rain. Rain water was also collected for the purpose of toilet flushing.

Relief to Eileen, for the pain she was suffering during her labour, wasn't a consideration. Giving birth was something that you simply got on with, and complained as little as possible about it. Kathy was almost as distressed as Eileen.

" Jaysus Mammy you got pregnant twice. How could you if it's this bad? Don't ever get the idea that I will make you a grandparent. Jaysus No, no, no, no, no."

Kathy didn't understand! Labour is a pain you forget about very quickly Kathy. Besides which in holy Ireland, contraception is not an option. You can't go to the local pharmacy and buy a packet of condoms, or get the morning after pill or see your doctor for the contraception pill. Those options simply are not available. We were all trying to conjure up ways of distracting my daughter so she couldn't hear the distress coming from the bottom room.

"Go into the kitchen Kathy and make us a cup of tea".

Keeping her busy might take up Kathy's thoughts. Kathy decided to tidy the cupboards. This wasn't a hard job, as like the rest of the house the kitchen was very basic, with a couple of small cupboards, and a sink for washing. She also went to the barns to check on the cows. A cow was in calf. Kathy volunteered to keep an eye on her. She lit the paraffin lamp to cast a glow, enough for her to see, but not so strong, that it upset the cow.

"Mammy come quickly the calf is here. There's a bloody mess everywhere. I do hope Eileen doesn't have that amount of blood loss".

I sent Padraig to the barns. There was nothing for him to do in the house except wait and listen to Eileen's screams from time to time. The idea of having your husband at your side was not an option. This was no place for men. Eileen had to see this through by herself, and of course the midwife, by now, was even more exasperated than when she arrived. Suddenly there was a commotion and then the bedroom door opened. Mrs Geary was standing in the doorway. She was looking very weary by now. There's no good news as yet. This poor woman has a long way to go, and there are complications. A cup of tea would be nice. She returned back to Eileen. Some forty minutes later there was an instruction from the bottom room

"Padraig go and send for the ambulance she bellowed. Tell them it's breach, tell them hurry."

Kathy went outside to the barns where Padraig was tending to the new calf. The calf was suckling its mother, looking safe happy and contented. Padraig had cleared away all the mess and looked worn out himself.

" I'm sorry Padraig there's complications with Eileen. Mrs Geary said you have to get an ambulance and tell them it's breach, and for god's sake hurry! Padraig wondered what that means. Jaysus Padraig I don't know. It doesn't matter what it means just do it and be quick".

 Padraig got his bicycle, and rode over the borreen, across the river, up the hill and then down the road to the post office which was four miles away. He would ask the postmaster to telephone for an ambulance.

"Jaysus will we ever see a second telephone in my life time".

Padraig was exasperated. Plumbing, piping, wiring Oh my god, surely those are basic things. If they can have them in Dublin, then why can't we have them here in the west? Life in the west and in particular in our parts was hard but people managed. After all, this is a family living in rural Ireland, in the early 1940s so in many ways the house was quite affluent, despite the lack of some facilities. The lack of facilities was more than compensated for though, by the scenic and idyllic setting. A river flowed gently, deep in parts, and shallow in others, at the bottom of the meadow, which was a distance of approximately ¾ of a mile from the house. Eileen and Kathy do the laundry in that river. This is our way of life

Four hours later, and who would have thought that it could take that length of time for an ambulance to arrive in such a dire situatuation. The ambulance was weaving its way down the borreen, just as Martin came into the world. A very troubled, long and difficult labour, eventually producing a small baby boy, with curls in his hair. A gentle at first and then getting louder cry emerged from the bottom room. He had a good set of lungs. Eileen was exhausted. She wanted to sleep. She held her son tightly for a few minutes, put him to the breast for a few minutes and then whilst she drank a very badly needed cup of tea, the baby was brought out of the room by Mrs Geary, and handed round to people as if he was a little parcel. Even the ambulance driver joined in with the excitement. Padraig was bursting with excitement. He hugged me, he hugged Kathy.

"Jaysus I'm a daddy "

The words were echoing through the house. Padraig went to the bottom room. I could hear my daughter crying. I could hear Padraig crying. They were crying and laughing at the same time. They were tears of joy, and bewilderment, all mixed in together. Eileen was glad she didn't have to go to the hospital. She knows how clinical it is there. This has strengthened her resolve, that she will return to her studies one day, and eventually be able to make changes herself when she's a qualified doctor.

"Merciful God "

Kathy screamed . It seems to be over at last. Such joy this family hadn't seen for a very long time. Four weeks later, the christening was going to be held. The white robe had been passed down through the generations. Eileen had decided many months ago, that she would ask her sister Kathy to be the godmother, and a cousin of Padraigs to be the godfather. Kathy was beside herself with excitement. Although she had known for some time that this would be happening the reality of it hadn't sank in with her.

"Me a godmother? She would tell to anyone who would listen. What huge responsibilities will that give to me? Will I be good enough? Will Martin like me as his second mammy?"

I tried to reassure my daughter. I wasn't sure that this was going to be possible though at that moment. Kathy was the type who needed lots of reinforcement where her abilities were concerned

"Its fine Kathy, you will be fine "

I just wish that your father was here to see this. To see our first grandchild. Kathy eventually settled down, and helped Eileen get Martin ready for bed. The christening day arrived. It was a wet day with some sunshine in between the showers. We all went in the cart. Barney was tied up outside the chapel until the service had finished. Kathy had prepared a small party for the family. A pig had been hanging at Michael's house for several weeks. The meat was awfully nice. I had made plenty of soda bread .Michael had brought a few bottles of Guinness as well as the port which was bought last Christmas. A few tunes were played on the flute. Eileen to my amazement did a couple steps of the double jig.

 "See mammy, I can still do it, having a baby hasn't changed any of that. I can't get the legs up, as high as I did before. Maybe that's because I'm getting older and nothing to do with the baby business".

Martins christening day turned out to be very special, and is one that will always be remembered by our family. Several weeks later the usual celebrations began again. Eileen and Padraig, well Eileen in particular, made the decision, that the house needed some music and some fun, they needed music and fun. Having a baby around the house, was fabulous, but not a reason, to put their own life's on hold. Every four weeks on a Saturday night the Flute playing and set dancing would continue till your legs were so tired, that you couldn't dance anymore, and sure the music would be soothing for the baby. It would help with the sleepless nights. Eileen had discovered the benefits of music, for a baby, whilst doing the paediatric side of her training. Now she was going to put it into practise. Martin got so much attention. So many people coming and going for the musical nights, and all of them wanting to fuss over the new baby. Eileen decided, that she would continue with her plan, to take one year off from her studies. This would be sufficient time to recover from the birth, to bond with her baby before she gave the shared care of him to her sister. A lot happened in that first year. The year went by very quickly. Martin had grown both physically and developmentally. He's not a clinging child and enjoyed the company of his extended family, especially Kathy's company.

" Kathy, you're like a second mammy to Martin. Sure one day you will have children of your own".

Kathy was uncertain about the possibility of that ever happening. She wasn't the most maternal person on this earth. She could remember clearly, the screams coming from the bottom bedroom on the night that Martin was born. She wasn't sure that she ever wished to have that experience herself. Eileen planned her breast feeding schedule very well. She had finished the weaning, from breast to bottle milk, just in time to resume her studies. The plans were in place. Everything would work out just fine

Eileen Returns To Medicine

The day of returning to Dublin arrived. It was a bright sunny day, so that made all of us, feel a little better. The dog was barking and birds singing away to their hearts content. Ducklings were running about outside waiting to be fed. The house was up early, 6am. Martin was cutting a tooth .He kept Eileen awake most of the night. She had made up a solution, from boiled nettle leafs mixed together with ginger. It was an old wife's tale, that if you rub it into the gums, it gives pain relief

"Jaysus Padraig, it's what my mammy always did, we have to try. The poor little lad is suffering far too much. There, there, now Martin shhhhhhhhh".

Eileen paced the room, holding the baby in her arms. Martin nodded off to sleep.

"Jaysus Padraig will you stop going on about it. I don't know, maybe it was the rubbing on the gums motion, maybe it was the walking, or maybe it was even the concoction itself. For Christ's sake I don't care. I'm just relieved that Martins not in pain anymore. I couldn't have bared to have gone to Dublin when he was suffering like that".

Eileen told her sister about the cure and what she should do if he's like that again. She knew that her husband didn't believe in it, therefore wouldn't put it in practise. Eventually she managed to get away for the nine o clock train. Padraig took her to the station. They rode horseback. See you tonight Padraig as she waved from the window of the train.

Eileen was travelling to Dublin daily. Two months on, and the early starts were telling on her. If only there were coffee machines, she would think to herself. The caffeine kick would help keep her alert. She had been caught cat napping, more than once, and was now on a final warning. Her future as a doctor was on the line! The train journey was always rough, and then, the long walk to the hospital was as much as she could manage. Eileen made a heart wrenching decision.

We were all back at the train station again, waving Eileen off, but this time, it was harder for her than she ever imagined. The daily commute had been too difficult, too tiring. She had decided that she would return home once every six weeks .She was going to live in residence in Dublin. A girl named Teresa, who worked with Eileen, and lived in Dublin, thought that it might be possible for her to rent a room from her parent's house. It was a tall building with few windows, on O Connell Street A busy street, even in them days, cars everywhere, even the odd bus. A picture house stood at the end of the road, and a coffee bar around the corner from the hospital where Eileen was on placement .The room she was renting was old fashioned. A single bed, no rug or carpet, just plain wooden floor, with a small sink in one corner, to get a wash, and a small chest in another corner, where Eileen placed her belongings. The family were very nice. Teresa had six sisters and two brothers. They were all excited, about having a stranger come to live in their house. The little ones wanted her to play in the garden with them. The older ones wanted her to go out to the dances with them. Eileen was torn. The family were so kind to her, she didn't want to offend, but at the same time she had so much studying to do, she didn't really have spare time for socialising very much. Teresa would often tell them to leave Eileen alone. Teresa had a good understanding of how busy she must be. Teresa's mammy would call from the hallway.

"Come down, and sit with us Eileen. It's not good to spend all that time on your own".

"I will be there in a minute I'm just finishing an essay".

This would be her second home for the following few years, she had to make the most of it. "It's lovely Teresa. I'll never forget you for this"

Over the years, she often went to chat with Teresa's mammy. Tell her all about Martin and how he was conceived out of wedlock. How her sister had judged her so badly and wanted her to go away.Teresas mammy was a very understanding, caring woman. She was able to help Eileen to see that whilst she didn't consider getting pregnant, out of wedlock to be anything that was bad, it was unfair that she would expect others to take the same view. Especially in holy Ireland where everyone says their prayers on bended knees at least twice daily. Eileen had kept deep hidden resentment to herself, in relation to how her sister had reacted. Now, it was as if a cloud had risen for her.

"Jaysus Helen you should be a councillor. I've never thought about it, in that way, before. I've tried, not to let Kathy see how much her opinions have affected me, but now, I have an understanding of why she reacted that way".

Eileen now began for the first time, to wonder how her mammy had really felt about the pregnancy. That night, she said special prayers, thanking the lord for everything good in her life and in particular her wonderful mother and sister. Eileen completed her term on the children's wards. So many sick children. Some would recover and some wouldn't. She remembered one little girl in particular. Her name was Alison. Alison was two years old, and a perfectly healthy and normal little girl, until the day that she was stricken down with Meningitis. Two years later, she had lost all of her hearing and was suffering from a degree of brain damage. Her parents were constantly on bended knees begging the lord for a cure for their daughter. Eileen persuaded them, to focus a little more on what was reality for them, and a little less on what she knew could never be. They joined a small group in Dublin that had been set up by Eileen, within the hospital, for children like Alison and their families. Slowly they began to accept the new life that was transforming in front of them. Eileen felt that she had helped that family for the rest of their life's.

"Doctor O Shaunessey is my child going to die? Is he, or she, going to suffer "?

Over and over again, those questions were asked, as she walked around the wards. Eileen found it heart wrenching. How can you tell a mother that her child won't be here soon, but she knew that if she wanted to be a doctor, then she needed to deal with this? She had to find a way to remind herself that whilst one side of the situation was painful, the other side when she could make a diagnosis and then treat it was helping. This is what would see her through the rest of her training days. Finishing her term on the children's wards was a huge relief. She had struggled a lot seeing so many mothers with their young children. It reminded her of her separation from her own child. She could hardly bare it. She sometimes struggled to keep focused on her work and not to wander off in her mind as to the well being of Martin. Was he missing her as much as she was missing him she often wondered? Would he recognise her on her return? Babies forget faces so quickly, she thought to herself. Eileen knew that she couldn't let those thoughts interfere with her work on the wards. She had to find ways to remain focused on her studies. She remembered the many promises which she had made to Kathy about the changes that she could hopefully bring about. She would keep those in her mind, to use as a distraction from her thoughts of Martin.

At the end of her day Eileen would stare through the window of her room. She often wondered what Padraig might be doing but mostly her thoughts were focused on her son. The baby rattle which had been made by his father sat on her pillow. This was the only connection she had with Martin, whilst she was in Dublin. Each day Eileen would tick off her calendar. Only one more year to go, then she would be back where she belonged.

Our family are very close, everyone helps out. My daughter Kathy had helped Padraig, take care of Martin, whilst Eileen finished her studying. Kathy is a bright girl too, but didn't have the same aspirations as her sister. In her school days Kathy would prefer to daydream, all day long, as opposed to listening to what she considered to be the most boring person ever put on this earth. Her mother's words, the words of her friends, the words of her teacher went round and round in her head

"You'll regret it one day Kathy"

It all fell on deaf ears. Many times Kathy was called to the front of the class, to explain her airy fairy attitude, to answer her teacher's accusations of what a disappointment she would one day, be to her mother.

Kathy knew different, she knew that her mother loved her regardless, and how, Why, would she ever consider her to be a disappointment. She never wanted Kathy to succeed for her, but of course she wanted it for Kathy. Success in life through Kathy's eyes was not being academic but finding happiness in other ways. She was in love, and this in itself was all the happiness that she desired. She would and did plan a very successful marriage. The sun shone all day long from getting up in the morning at 6am, to help milk the cows, right through to falling into bed at 11pm that night. Yes even on her wedding day that was the way of life. Kathy was a very down to earth type of girl. Working the farm, to her on her special day, was like me and you making a cup of tea. Jimmy O Donovan was in disbelief

"Go away with ya Kathy. Sure you haven't been working on the farm this morning".

"Oh be Jaysus now Jimmy, sure you're a townie yourself. What would you know about country life? If you knew anything at all, you wouldn't be surprised".

Kathy looked like a princess in her new dress, bought specially for the occasion. The sale at Mulligan's is always good in the summer. Friend's family and neighbours gathered at the small church. The same church that refused to marry her sister. Kathy is a forgiving kind of person, and anyway, she sort of understood why the priest had refused Eileen. A distant cousin gave her away. Kathy wondered what her father would say if he was alive. He never forgave the

McGeevers, for getting ahead of him at the fair, and securing the purchase of the prize bull, which he had an eye on for a very long time and now his daughter, is marrying into that very same family. Kathy and Michael went to visit the cemetery before returning home after their marriage ceremony.

"Well mammy we did it. Me and Kathy. We made you proud. Today we got married, and we know, that you were there with us, even though we couldn't see you". The McGeever family have had more than their fair share of trouble. They also went to talk to Kathy's father. His grave looked unkept. Weeds growing all around. Kathy got upset she pulled the weeds away with her bare hands. They stayed longer than they had planned to. There was so much to tell him, she told him all about Eileen and the baby and the marriage to Padraig and of course her own marriage to Michael.

" Come on Kathy it's time to go"

Michael took hold of his wife's hand, and led her back to the road, where a friend was waiting to take them home. A small gathering was held, back at the house...A few stouts, and woodbines (Booze and Fags) were passed around. A few hornpipes danced away the night, with Jimmy on the Flute, and Michael, getting carried away, with his rendition of his rebel songs and in particular, the wild colonial Boy. How he ever got the grip of singing, and actually knowing some of the words, was beyond my level of understanding. Michael would always sing, when he had a few stouts inside him, and had no concern about the sound of his voice. He would sign at the same time. It almost felt like, if he was signing the words, then that would help others understand the sound he was producing. A big clap went up when he had finished. Everyone admired Michael, for his level of confidence and determination. Michael wished that his mammy could have been there, to see him marry Kathy, but alas, life sometimes is very cruel.

Kathy, since marrying Michael Mc Geever, enjoys the simplicity of life without the stresses of outside employment. She is not in the slightest bit envious of her sister's career. In some ways, she feels that maybe Eileen should envy her, for the almost, stress free life she lives, helping Michael to run the farm. The following months saw Kathy and Michael settle down into married life. A life that would hopefully bring many good things for them and to them.

Eileen had reached the end of her term at Dublin University. At last she would be back in the bosom of her home and her family. She looked forward to the many hours that she would be able to spend with Martin. She decided that she would have a few months at least before she attempted to find a job. Studying to be a doctor was something that with a lot of encouragement from Dr O Brien, she had begun to dream of throughout her years at school. The past what should have been six years, but due to life events turned into eight, had gone by, much faster than she ever anticipated. The months from finishing at Dublin, had gone faster than she hoped they would. She was now looking forward to combining her position as the new doctor, with spending precious time with her Son, and of course being a wife to Padraig. Padraig O Shaunessey married to a doctor. He had struggled with this concept right from the beginning. In fact I have often wondered if Padraig had hoped that the pregnancy would have been enough to make Eileen decide that she couldn't continue with her desire to practise medicine. In his eyes this is not women's work. Padraig began to withdraw a little from her. He began to spend some time in the local bar, especially on the day of the fair being held. He was beginning to feel threatened, by the success, enjoyed by his wife. He does however, realise, that Eileen has the determination to succeed and live her life as she wishes.

This area needs a new doctor. At 78, it's a strain for Dr O Brien to continue in his practise. Dear Dr O Brien. A stocky man with greying hair, and a great sense of humour. He's seen many changes in our village, stuck many needles into the arms of screaming children. Now he's feeling that maybe the time is right for him to consider handing over to fresh blood. Many a time he has told Eileen, that one day she would be sitting in his chair. Eileen enjoyed the challenges her new position gave her, enjoyed coming home at the end of each long day to be with her son. To hear his attempts at relaying the events of the day to her. To hold him in her arms, and throw him in the air, just like she remembered and loved her father to do to her.Oh God, Eileen missed her father. She cried and cried the day he went to Castlebar, as the ambulance moved slowly down the borreen.

"Oh mammy will he ever come back? Tell me! Will he? Will he? "

Eileen was only eleven when her father was struck down with pneumonia .The hospital was far away, was small, with few facilities. I went mostly on my bicycle to see him. I didn't take the children. John was very weary, and tired looking. He was struggling to breathe. He extended his arm towards me He took hold of my hand.

"Jaysus Biddy I wish that I never saw them bloody fags".

He used my name. John had never in his life, except the day that we were married, called me by my name, and now, here he is on his death bed, being affectionate. He was in the hospital for three weeks, before we got the telegram. The doctors did all they could, but it wasn't enough. John was a very well known and much liked, by everyone, type of man. People came from far and near to celebrate the life, and to mourn the death of my husband. The girls were very distressed. Kathy in particular had no real understanding of what had happened. After the pain of losing her father, and even though she was only eleven when it happened Eileen knew, that if medical knowledge was improved then there would have been a better chance of his survival. She decided that this was going to strengthen her resolve to practise medicine.

Eileen without Padraigs blessing, decided to have another musical night, so that everyone could say goodbye to Dr O Brien, and to welcome her to her new position. Friends and neighbours arrived as did both families. Dr O Brien arrived a little late. He had brought a gift for Eileen.

" I always saw you sitting in this chair Eileen, even when you were a little girl, now it's all yours and Jaysus you don't half deserve it. Your family must be so proud of you. The village is so proud of you. May you be the doctor here for many a long year to come".

The cheers and claps were resounding. Eileen was filled with confidence, filled with excitement. This was going to be one of the best nights of her life. The reels and jigs could be heard pounding through the walls. Padraig struggled. His jealous feelings became fairly evident, when he suggested to his wife.

" Eileen you sit by my side for the rest of the evening, and stop talking to the neighbours, and to Emanon O Hara in particular."

Padraig had sensed something, had felt a degree of insecurity in the presence of Eamonn. He didn't like the way in which Eamonn looked at Eileen, he felt threatened by it. He felt inferior to his wife, although Eileen is the last person who would ever knowingly make anyone feel that way. This was Padraigs problem and nothing to do with anything that my daughter had done. Surely he should have known that his wife would never be manipulated, would never be told how to behave. This unknown to them and with an unforeseeable event in the future would be the last celebration in this house. There's a gloomy feel about this home now, no more dancing, no more flute playing the Sligo reel. Eileen and Padraig are of course getting older, but, Jesus, Mary and Joseph that's not the reason why the fun has left those walls. Neither, is it because of the introduction of the dance hall act which tried to close down all the house dances .Father John is the most regular visitor to the house these days, and has been so, over the past 4- 5 years.

The birth of my other grandchildren was a little less traumatic, than that of their brother Martin. Padraig, Eileen and even Kathy, were much more prepared and not so anxious. Finance wasn't such a concern, as they already had the crib and pram, and a collection of baby clothing from Martin. Kathy was very supportive and helped Eileen throughout the weeks of her pregnancies. She would often take Seamus to her home for overnight stays, so that Eileen could rest. The weeks seemed to drag on and on. Eileen became a little depressed when she discovered that the middle one wasn't going to be especially easy. Annette had been lying in the breech position for several weeks and just as Eileen had given up hope of another home delivery the baby turned by itself. Seamus, Annette, and Eefie, were very much welcomed into our family. They brought many a joyous moment to my daughter and the occasional smile to the face of their father Padraig. School life was hard for them, especially for Seamus, when he was taunted about his red hair. The curls were flowing just like his mothers. How he wished he could have it cropped off.

"Be Jaysus Seamus sure it's a fine head you have there"

The resistance coming from his father was not welcomed by Seamus, but he knew his Da well enough, to know that for now, there's no choice. The many restrictions placed unfairly on the children were also a source of aggravation for them. They craved a normal family life, but Padraig couldn't, wouldn't, allow this to happen. The only sense of real normality they experienced would be, when they stayed at their Aunt Kathy's home overnight. The walk to school by yourself restriction, on Seamus, was lifted

"I don't have the time Eileen and sure he's a fine boy, well able to go to school on his own.

Eileen always saw through her sister's defence but also secretly agreed with her, therefore she didn't object. Eileen was unable to stand up to her husband in the day to day care of their children, so the requests to Kathy for the children, and Seamus in particular, became more and more frequent, for them to stay over. Everyone always forgot to tell Padraig that Kathy had such a busy life, therefore confrontation was reduced.

"I love the freedom Aunt Kathy".

The teasing at school would stop when the kids saw Seamus running across the fields by himself. His heart ached for this to be a normal part of his home life.

"Jaysus Aunt Kathy, can't you talk to my parents".

Kathy's heart was wishing that she could. She had on previous occasions attempted this conversation to Padraig. It fell on deaf ears. Eileen was always more accepting of what Kathy had to say, but alas, without the blessing of her husband there wouldn't be any movement in the way that the children were restricted. Whilst in Kathy's care, Seamus was thrilled to have the opportunity to be able to walk to his friend's house in the next village, picking berries from the hedgerows, and sharing the details of the flute that had been given to him by Jimmy O Donavan. He loved his music and showed a real talent. Those rare events were so looked forward to by Seamus. The girls were growing too, and wanting a little independence, but still young enough to be accepting, without too much question, the decision made by their parents and in particular by their father. They were yet to discover just how restricted and smothered their lives would become. The family dogs. Well they are something else. On the one hand, they would be obedient working animals and in the next breath they were playful with the children, enthusiastic when in their role as guard dogs. Their living quarters would vary depending on the whereabouts of Padraig. The poor dogs suffered such confusion, never really sure of where they should be, or what was required from them. Spotty would cower in a corner when Padraig entered its space. He has on more than one occasion felt the wrath of Padraigs anger. Padraig like his father before him, in his younger day, (he's ten years older than Eileen) was a worker in the building trade, therefore found that the building of his own home, was a challenge he would enjoy. Knowing people in the trade, together with the money from his accident, had helped with the cost of materials. Padraig had a good brain; he was able to design the layout for the new house. Friends and family joined in, to help with the construction of the house. They did this without any monetary gain to themselves. This was the way of life. This house, could only be described as a luxury of the early 1940s in a rural Irish village, where life was so incredibly simple, yet so hard, but no one   complained

Finance For The New House

Padraig had some spare time on his hands. There wasn't very much doing on the farm. The weather was dismal as usual. He could have dug out, half a field of potatoes, to sell at the market the following week, but choose instead, to take the day off. He decided to surprise Eileen. He would go to Dublin to see her. He imagined the look on her face, when she answered her front door, and he would be standing there. Padraig always had a very vivid imagination. He got out his best shirt and a pair of trousers that maybe had seen better days. He thought about wearing the trousers which Eileen had bought specially as a treat for him. She found them in the sale in a rather posh shop in O Connell Street in Dublin. Padraig decided that she wouldn't be best pleased as they were intended for special occasions. Kathy appeared from round the side of the house.

"Jaysus Padraig your looking smart, what's the craic?"

Padraig explained that he was going to Dublin and the story about the trousers.

"Be Jaysus Padraig, you going to see my sister at the hospital, couldn't be more special than that".

Padraig got changed again. He put on the trousers Eileen had bought for him. Kathy drove the horse and cart to Balla for the eleven O clock connection to Dublin. He spent his time daydreaming whilst waiting for the train to arrive. He remembered the many occasions that he had taken Eileen to this very station. A lump began to grow in his throat, as he remembered the tears in her eyes, when he squeezed her so tightly; she thought that she might burst. Oh, how he loved his Eileen, how he missed her loving ways, her gentle touch. He longed to be with her. To hold her in his arms again. The train left promptly at 11am, chugging its way across the middle of Ireland. Padraig watched out through the windows, and then he fell asleep. This was his first trip to Dublin. Eileen had told him what it was like, however Padraig hadn't really got the picture. The train station in Dublin was much bigger than he imagined. City life and the volume of road traffic, is something he was not used to. He was feeling a little anxious as well as excited about what lay ahead. One bottle of stout to settle his nerves, from the shop on O Connell Street won't do any harm Padraig told himself. Be Jaysus it will calm the jitters. Of course for Padraig it never stops at one.

He chuntered to himself, as he hurried between the motorcars, whilst attempting to cross O Connell Street. The cars were coming very fast. Padraig panicked, should he go back, or should he go forward, or should he simply stand still. It was too late. A much disorientated Padraig woke in the hospital. Events of that day were erased from his memory. The pain was severe. Confusion was immense. Padraig attempted to move. His cries were heard in the next ward. The nurse, a middle aged lady named Nora, with greying hair and a wrinkly face, in her flowing white gown, and matching hair cap, was cowering over his bed changing the dressing on his leg.

"Be quiet Padraig she cried. Sure you'll upset everyone on the ward". "

"You know my name. How do you know my name? What's happened? Where am I?"

The questions were coming fast and thick from an impatient Padraig. Again he tried to get off the bed. The pain sent him right back down.

" Just be quiet Padraig. Let me do my job, and then I will tell you all about it, tell you the whole long story."

The nurse washed both of his legs, above and below the dressings, and put a clean bandage on the cuts on his arm. Padraig felt like he had no choice, once again he screamed out in pain

"Jesus, Mary and Joseph help me "

Padraig blessed himself with the sign of the cross. That's better said Nora. You ask the lord God for help, and he will calm you. She sprinkled some holy water over his body.

" There now, I could get the sack if I'm seen doing this, so you don't say a word."

Padraig was worn out by the intensity of the pain, and the after effects of the anaesthetic. He drifted off to sleep and woke two hours later .Nora explained about the accident and how Padraig had been brought into the hospital by two young men who were in Dublin on that day.

"Jaysus Padraig you are lucky not to be dead. The angels must have been watching down on you"

Padraig wasn't one to believe such rubbish, but he did consider how true her statement was, in relation to him being dead. The metal plate would be removed in a further operation to happen in six months time. Three weeks later, and on Eileen's weekend to go home, Padraig was collected in a car, provided by the neighbours back in Mayo. The car driver was fast. The roads were in poor condition. He was sick on the homeward journey. He wondered, how he could have been so stupid, to have got himself, into that situation in the first place. For the second operation, he had a choice of going to Castlebar or going back to Dublin. Padraig thought to himself, that Eileen has always praised the Dublin hospital. It turned out that Eileen was on theatre duty, on the day his operation was due to take place. This was considered to be a bad idea

"You know better Eileen you can't assist an operation on your own friends or family"

The words were bellowed out by Mr McGinty, the head surgeon in that Hospital. Eileen changed her shift and had the day off instead, so that she could be with Padraig when he came round from the anaesthetic. There now, she wiped his forehead and helped him to sit forward, when he needed sips of water to quench his thirst. Eileen is a very compassionate type of person. She would have made a very good nurse. Padraig made a full recovery, and returned back home two weeks later. The driver, who knocked him down in O Connell Street, had been drinking, and didn't stop after the accident. The two young men in who brought Padraig into the hospital had witnessed what had happened. They were very quick thinking young men. They made a note of the registration. The men were colleagues of Eileen's which explains how they knew Padraigs name. The Garda are very serious, in hit and run matters. Padraig was awarded a substantial amount of compensation. He and Eileen made the decision that the money would provide them with a smart new house where they could raise a family.

Back On The Farm

Padraig and Eileen were very self sufficient with their small holding, forty acres, plus four acres of bog land. Being raised on a farm is a blessing that we don't appreciate when we have it all. The sounds of nature, from when you get up in the morning, till you go to bed at night are so soothing and idyllic. Life here is, although very busy on the one hand, lived in the slow lane on the other hand. Sure there are things to get done but to be done in one's own time. Many a hard day's work has been had in the fields. Mowing the hay, and building the hayricks. Digging the turf, and rounding up the cows at the end of each day. The thrashing of the corn was a day that all the neighbours looked forward to. Padraig and Eileen would always take a picnic, with special treats for the children who came along to watch. Everyone in the village mucked in. The thrashing machine was hired for a small fee, from a man in the next village. Occasionally an animal would be lost. The sadness of losing a cow or two in the trenches was something that all the farmers had to endure .The neighbours would all join in, when there's a rescue going on. I'm remembering one occasion in particular. The trench was deep. Padraig fetched the ropes. The men pulled and tugged again and again. The rescue was lost. It was devastating for them to lose an animal. The children would be distraught, in the knowledge that an animal had suffered such a horrible death. Padraig and Eileen, whilst sharing the feelings of their children, had the added burden that this was part of their income, an income they could not afford to lose. Eileen was always able to manage to put a positive slant on things. It was a skill that she had developed over the years also a part of her personality.

"Jaysus Padraig sure worse things than this happen .At least we have each other and our family and most importantly our health. We have a great future to look forward to. No more moping around about this situation"

Milk being prepared for the creamery, and bread baking on the open fire, was a daily chore that the children loved to help with. They enjoyed watching the milk in the churn, going round and round, eventually turning into a slab of butter. These chores were performed before the school day started and again in the evenings after school. Income from the milk is small but it all adds up. Cattle, pigs, sheep and poultry were the bulk of their stock. The children loved to chase the chicks and goslings across the yard and to gather eggs from the nests. The sound of the cockerel could be heard each morning, throughout the village.

The local Bull has been kept busy, four of Padraigs cows are now in calf, which will provide the family with some income for the following year, however it's debateable as to how this income will be distributed. It doesn't always go where it should if you know what I mean.

Padraig had been to the market. It started off, a dull, and dreary wet day. Throughout the morning the clouds broke up, the sun began to shine. Padraig knew that this increased the chances of selling his stock. People were more likely to travel in the better weather. A fine market it was .Farmers came from miles away. You can now almost hear the silence, coming from the pig house, as most of the sows have now gone. I can't help wondering how he has spent the money, but am sure that I can guess, and I feel confident that my dear daughter Eileen, will not have seen very much of it. Donovan's bar where the flute playing is the best you have ever heard, will probably have been propping him up, as that's Padraigs usual watering hole on market days, and any other day when there's a penny in his pocket. Eileen seems to have lost her will, and her ability to assert herself, to her husband in order to assure that she has the money she needs to keep the home going. Despite my many requests, to Jimmy Donavan, to recognise an alcoholic when he sees one, Padraig is still one of his most welcomed customers. Jimmy, a middle aged man has been raised with alcohol. His father before him, ran the pub, was an alcoholic himself, and has two brothers, who are alcoholics. He does nothing to discourage the people who seriously shouldn't be drinking. All Jimmy appears to think about is how much money is going into his pockets. I often wonder if that man has a conscience at all.

Martins Accident

The death of his first born, at age, three years, is something Padraig blames himself for. This blame, this guilt, has taken its toll on every aspect of Padraig, his life, his family. Padraig had been fishing Trout was the usual Friday night meal, so just like he did every Friday, Padraig collected his bucket from the kitchen, and waited very impatiently whilst Eileen prepared his lunch.

" Jesus, Mary and Joseph, Eileen, he yelled, you haven't made me sandwiches yet"

Eileen gave him the bag. Ham from the pig that had been hanging, lettuce and tomatoes with shallots from the garden. A bottle of tea to help wash it all down. He was in a bad temper. Padraig didn't appreciate being kept waiting. He grabbed the bag from her hand. He didn't even say "Thank you"

"Oh for god's sake Padraig, maybe you should try getting your own sandwiches. Who makes them for me or for anyone else round here? Everyone does their own, except you, so yes maybe you should consider that fact and show a little gratitude at least"

Padraig was surprised by his wife's reaction. It wasn't what he had become used to. Eileen was forever the dutiful wife. Maybe now she was going to say that enough is enough. Padraig left for the afternoon, he walked through the meadows, to reach the stream where he would do his bare hand fishing. Spring has been fairly good weather wise, also early summer, so now the grass is high. Eileen had called after him that Martin was also going to the river. Eileen went inside the house. The dresser needed cleaning. That's what she would do today, and then go to Balla on her bicycle. Eileen loved her bicycle. We had given it to her, for her 10th Birthday. The saddle was adjustable and it had a carrying seat on the back. Eileen often took Martin on the bicycle for rides around the village. Martin followed his father to the river. He was short for his age, his tiny body almost covered by the long grass. Padraig hadn't heard his wife, he didn't realise that his son was following him. Padraig sat in silence waiting to see a movement by the large stones in the stream. His thoughts, which should have been on the safety of his child, were on the forthcoming Hurley match, to be played a week on Saturday. Would Roscommon win again he wondered? He hoped not, as Mayo, has had a very bad Hurley season and needed this forthcoming game on their table.

Martin adored his father, and had been following him to the river, ever since he took his first steps at the age of fourteen months. He loved to roll about in the long grass and listen to nature. He was playing near the embankment. A mischievous, cute looking child, the image of his father, with red curly hair, and a face full of freckles even at the age of three. He would squeal with delight, every time he saw Padraig collect the bucket and walk towards the river He didn't understand what his father was doing, he was curious, he wandered to the river edge. The bank was unsettled from the recent bad weather, which we see so much of. Our village will never experience a drought, that's for sure. In a split second, Martin was sliding down the embankment, he was in the stream. Padraig heard the surge of water splashing. He looked up quickly, to see his son laying there, his little face covered by the water. By the time that his father reached him he had drowned. A frantic and screaming Padraig pulled him out lifeless and still.

"Oh my god. Eileen, how do I tell Eileen?"

Padraig ran back to the house screaming. Having to face his wife was the last thing he wanted to do! How would he tell her? What would she say? Would she hold him responsible? Padraig arrived back at the front door. Eileen was in the top field. She could hear his screams from the distance, piercing in her ears. Padraig collapsed to the ground .He struggled to get the words out. Eileen was in disbelief. She calmly walked down the field back inside the house. The shock was too much for her. She carried on cleaning the dresser, like nothing had happened.

"Jaysus Eileen will you stop that and sit down".

Michael had been walking over the meadow at the same time as Padraig came rushing back. Michael's voice was calm and serene unlike the usual coarseness it has. It was almost as though he was able to control the quality of his speech when the situation called for it. He held Eileen tightly and told her that Padraig was on the ground outside. I'm not sure of the events that followed those moments. That evening a neighbour, got a car from Balla, and took all of us to the chapel. We said prayers that Padraig and Eileen might be comforted in their tragic loss. The whole village was in mourning. I will never forget, the locals will never forget, the sadness, and turmoil brought upon all of us. No one blamed Padraig; however, Padraig blamed, and never forgave himself, for the events of that dark and gloomy day. On his many sessions of reflection Padraig will occasionally express his feelings

"I should have known that Martin had followed me. I shouldn't have been so angry and should have been listening to my wife. Martin always follows me when I go to the river. My thoughts should have been on my son and not on the forthcoming Hurley match"

The dreaded day

The sun was shining. At least they didn't have the torrents of the weather to get through. Padraig and Eileen were up early, about half past four. Kathy and Michael helped with the milking that morning. Eileen cried and cried in her bedroom, for at least an hour, before coming out for a cup of tea.

"Some soda bread Eileen or a slice of brack"

She nodded her head. Eileen's medical training was helping her, to get through this. She knew that she had to keep her energy levels up. She struggled with the second slice, and the egg that Kathy had fried for her. Padraig was huddled in the corner. He too ate breakfast, albeit not like he usually would. I had never before, or since that day, seen my daughter so visibly distressed. Martin's tiny coffin lay on the floor in their bedroom. The lid was kept open till about an hour before they had to leave the house. The family gathered around looking at his tiny face. They recited the rosary over and over. They sprinkled his body with holy water. Padraig closed the lid. Silence fell upon the room.

The journey to the Chapel seemed like a very long one. Padraig, Eileen, Michael, Kathy and I all took it in turns to carry the tiny coffin. As we weaved our way through the villages, the houses were empty. Everyone joined the procession to the chapel. Eventually we got there at eleven, for the funeral service at eleven fifteen, and burial at half past one in the afternoon. Cups of tea and a tray of woodbines were passed around that evening back home. People kept dropping in, to offer their condolences. Over the following weeks, Eileen decided that she had to get some good from this tragic situation. She had to get her positive attitude back somehow. She decided that everything happens for a reason. That god wanted Martin for his own purpose and she was going to respect that. Eileen decided that her community needed her. She returned back to her position as the local doctor. In the best way that she could, she got on with her life. Padraig did not have her strength of character. He neglected the farm, neglected his wife and family. He spent hours, and days and months, and even years, wrapped up in self pity. Martin was his main topic of conversation

" Be Jaysus Padraig, it's been a few years now, you have to move on. People won't want to keep hearing it."

Eileen's words didn't sink in. Martin was all he could think about, he became obsessed and made no immediate effort to change the way he was. Over time, things improved in some ways, to some degree, and in other ways things deteriorated. The fact, that Eileen and Padraig, had gone on, to have more children, had brought some degree of joy to the house.

Seamus Confronts His Parents

Seamus is the eldest of my grandchildren. At almost 14, he towers above his sisters. Padraig, in the past had made a mistake with his first born Martin. This mistake is now shaping the way in which my grandchildren are allowed to live their lives.

"Jaysus mammy, I am thirteen you know"

Seamus screamed at his mother, as he attempted to walk to school, by himself, or alone with his sisters, through the meadows, over the bridge, which covers the very spot where the events of a certain day many years ago would shape the lives of the Shaughnesssy family for ever more. The regular trips to the cemetery seem a little unfair to Seamus, when yet again he has had to say no to his school friend, when invited to go blackberry picking or, bare hand fishing, or any other activity the local children seemed to do. Seamus is frustrated by the boundaries imposed on him by his parents but in particular by Padraig. Seamus behaved badly on a fairly regular basis. Some days he would have tantrums that you could only associate with a two year old. Other times his challenges were more age appropriate, with him going out and staying at neighbours homes. Seamus would have a tale to tell which allowed him to stay and not go home for days. On a few occasions I found him chasing the chicks and killing them needlessly, Stealing bottles of stout from Donovan's and getting drunk.

"Jaysus Seamus if the Garda catch you, you're in trouble .Jimmy Donovan was worried .Maybe I should tell your Da. Your mothers a doctor, why doesn't she notice and see what's happening to her child?"

Seamus, his head buried in his hands, cried so many tears like he had never cried in his life. He felt helpless. He knew that it was a hopeless situation and would probably always be like that.

" It's no good, they will never change, never let me have a normal life."

Seamus felt alone. He had no one to talk too. Jimmy was willing to listen, but not that he really cared. Jimmy's concern in the main, was, that if Seamus should be caught drunk by the Garda he might tell them where he got the stout. He might say that Jimmy gave it to him. Seamus was having feelings of despair. His brother was dead and now he has to live his life, based on that fact. The unfairness of it all was too much for him.

Seamus made a decision. As soon as he reached fourteen he would be off. He told Eefie and Annette. His sisters were distraught, by the thought of their brother leaving, and by the fact that they couldn't tell their parents, well not yet anyhow.

"I have to Eefie.I have to go".

Eeefie and Annette cried all night long. There was no consoling them. Their brother was leaving. He was sailing to England.

"What life have I got here? It's a desperate situation. I help in the bogs. Make the hayricks. Go to school, and never out of the sight of my father. It's not normal".

Seamus picked his moment. He told his parents the news. The fair day had just been. McCalpines Fusiliers had descended at the fair in Kiltimagh, recruiting workmen for the building trade in Britain. Seamus had signed up to go. He would do a few months with Mc Calpines and then see how things were. See if he felt there was any movement from his father.Padraig hung his head down. He begged Seamus to change his mind. He promised him that he would stop drinking and not be so violent to their mother and to the children. He made no acknowledgement that he was suffocating his children by his over protective attitude

" It's no good da. You smother me. I'm going away and that's that. I'm going to go to London and anyway, didn't you raise me for export? That's surely what happens in most families here in the west of Ireland. Everyone leaves for England or America when they get to my age".

Seamus suddenly seemed so knowledgeable, so mature, to his father. He was assertive in a very polite way.

"You don't know me, not really know me! I love music; I love the flute and tin whistle. You didn't know that did you? I'm just thirteen years old, I'm your son and you didn't know that I love music. You're not interested in me, only really interested in the past and your own guilty feelings. I hate you. Seamus was angry now. I steal, I drink stout and then I kill the chickens. You don't even notice".

Padraig collapsed back into his chair. The boy in front of him was almost a man and Padraig hadn't noticed how grown up he had become.

" Yes, I will work for Mc Calpines to start with, in Manchester, and then maybe when I get to London, someone will help me get work in the Irish bars .I can play you know. When you hear the flute music from behind the bushes you always say that it's the tinkers on their travels. Well it isn't Pa it's me. Yes it's me secretly playing the flute, and knowing that I could never tell you, because we are not allowed to have pleasure. Jimmy Donovan gave me the flute. Even he knew that I couldn't tell you. Everybody knows that you don't let us have a normal life. You think that you let our brother drown, and now we have to suffer for it."

Seamus was bitter. He felt the unfairness of it all.

"Yes Da you think I'm stupid you think that I don't know what happened to Martin, well I do and I know that you think that it was your fault. Jimmy told me. Jaysus Da everyone knows, and everyone agrees that it's not fair that we have to suffer because of a mistake that was made so many years ago. Yes Da a mistake, which was no one's fault, so stop blaming yourself for Christ sakes, and let your children have a life."

Padraig had never in his life, shut up for so long and let one of his children speak for as long as they wanted to without their father's interruptions. Phew! Seamus was exhausted. He almost shocked himself by the way he had challenged his father. Had he gone too far, had he said too much to his father or was he absolutely right to have confronted him this way, as its destroying all their lives. He told himself that yes he had done the right thing. He owed it to himself and also to his sisters. After all, they are younger than him. They can't stand up for themselves. They will have very restricted lives when they are older just like he does. Eefie had been listening. She cowered down behind Padraigs chair. The noise of her sniffles and quiet sobs gave it away. Eeefie was frightened. She never heard her brother so angry before and having an argument with their father.

"Don't cry Eefie it's all right. Come here let me hug you. You're too young to understand those things but you will understand when you're older"

Seamus was showing a maturity beyond his years. He had grown up very quickly right in front of his parents eyes and they didn't notice. Eefie had no idea how gentle her brother could be. She had never seen him this angry; she had never seen him this gentle

Padraig was shocked. It showed in his face. He was speechless. He went back to his chair and opened a bottle of stout. That was Padraigs answer to everything

"So much for cutting out drinking Da. I knew you wouldn't do it. I knew it."

Padraig carried on like nothing had been said, he ignored his son's comments. The next few hours saw Padraig have one bottle after another until he was so drunk that he was not able to stand up. Seamus decided that if he ever had any doubt about his decision to leave that doubt had definitely been removed.

Eileen Sees the Devastation

Eileen felt so guilty. As usual, she tried to hide her emotions but the strain was too much. She asked herself .What have we done to our three children"? This can't go on. Eileen would have to talk to Padraig, she would have to make him see sense. She would make him understand that what happened to Martin was an accident and that they can't continue to allow it to impact on the other children anymore than it already has done. Eefie who's nearly nine is a very quiet child. Her long hair, full of curls, and almost as red as her Mothers is usually tied in a ponytail. She does fairly well at school from an academic point of view. Children do talk to her in the playground. She doesn't have any friends coming to the house. Eileen wished that Eefie would have some dry nights. It would boost her confidence. Help her to feel a bit more grown up. The regular bed wetting is more to do with the unrealistic boundaries, and her lifestyle, than the fact that she says

"But the bedroom is so cold it makes me want to pee, and I'm too frightened of the dark, frightened to get out of bed and use the lavatory."

She's a small girl for her age. Padraig never allows her to play in the meadow.

"The grass is so long Eefie, we won't know where you are ".

Padraig is paranoid. Eileen has had enough. She decided that she has to tackle this now. It can't go on any longer. Padraig needs help.

"Oh my God, Jaysus Padraig, its seventeen years now, the children have to have a life"

Eileen was exasperated with him, and now Seamus will be going soon. Eileen was wondering would Annette be next, she's eleven now and is head strong already. Annette has the personality of her mother with a determination to match. Eileen is taking a much closer look at all her children, and how they are being affected.

"Why don't your friends come over to play Annette?"

Annette wasn't brave enough to be honest. How could she tell her mother that everyone thinks they are weird? That she no longer has any friends, because she can never go out, and do stuff with them. That her bullying father is almost always drunk to some degree, so why would she even think about asking friends over, if she had any that is. Then she changed her mind. Why shouldn't she let people know the truth? The determination she has demonstrated in every other aspect of her life would now prove to be a valuable asset for her. She decided that she would be totally honest with her mammy.

Eileen picked the time to talk to Padraig, about the children, very carefully. It was an evening after a good day in the fields. Eileen had cooked a hearty meal for the whole family. Eileen took Padraig outside. They sat on a bench sipping a cup of tea . She began by reminiscing, about her own upbringing, and that of Padraigs also. He acknowledged how much he had enjoyed his own childhood. He remembered the hardships endured by his parents, for one reason or another. His mind was now clearly fixed on family life and the good upbringing of children. Eileen felt, that when she tackled the issue of their children, it was probably going to go quite well. She was wrong! She was disappointed. Padraig was not listening to her. He had no intention of letting his children have the freedom they deserve. He's become a very selfish man, who only gives consideration to his own needs and feelings. The children are well aware that they have a brother in Heaven, and speak of him often, although they have no idea what he looked like. Padraig and Eileen had never managed to get a photograph of their first born Son.

My Visit

As I entered the house, Padraig was sitting in his usual place. He is now, a middle age man, with a middle age spread to match. His handsome face never changing, despite the way he abused his body with alcohol. You would hear the noise coming from his throat a mile away, as he slept through his own thunder storm. When Padraigs snoring, a thunder storm is exactly what he sounds like. Two empty stout bottles, on the floor next to his chair, whilst my now, down trodden daughter, was once again, being the best she could be, and preparing to entertain for the evening.

Jackie and Eamon have been friends with Eileen and Padraig for a long time. I never really understood the friendship, as Jackie is so different to my daughter and why Eamon would ever want to be in the same house as Padraig I will never know. I sort of decided that it wasn't my business to understand and left them to get on with the friendships the wanted, or at least thought they wanted. Maybe there were more underlying reasons for Eamon wanting to be there. There's a meal planned for this evening. Jackie would be arriving shortly. No doubt that she would be drenched in the most recent perfume from the shelves in New York. Eamon would follow later, when the weeks marking is finished. Eamon teaches at the local school .He makes his work a priority in his life, going nowhere until it's completed. Generous as ever Eamon had purchased some jewellery for his wife. He had given his secretary some money and a request to choose something that Jackie would like. Eamon decided that she had spent wisely. You made a good choice at that new jewellers shop on O Connell Street . Susie had done the shopping whilst she was in Dublin to see her Grandchildren. Her time there had been a badly needed and well deserved break. Susie was a middle aged, very hard working woman who supported Eamon in most aspects of his life and who doted on her Grandchildren. Many a time she told Eamon how she wished that her Son had stayed local and not followed his friends to Dublin. How she missed the regular contact with her Grandchildren and watching them growing up. Going to Dublin was never an easy task for Susie. She had Arthritis in one knee so the long bus journey with all that sitting down, didn't do her any favours. Eamon looked at the dangling earrings again and again.

"Jackie will love them. You sure I gave you enough Susie? they look far more expensive than £3."

I often wish that Padraig might be a little more, no a lot more, like Eamon, who appears to adore his wife, and treats her with such respect, despite the fact that it's not reciprocated. I'm confident that Eamons playing the game. Made his bed, now he has to lie on it, rather than want to continue to lie on it .If he truly cared that much for his wife, surely he wouldn't send his secretary to choose her presents.

Seamus, Eefie and Annette, were sitting quietly at the table made from logs collected from the Oak trees at the back of the house. Beautiful trees, with their wide, outstretching branches, having stood there for the past 100 years or so. On many an occasion, the trees had been used as goal posts in practice sessions, by Mikey Donovan. Mikey was the newest recruit to Roscommon town, who coincidentally, beat Mayo, by two nil last week. Hurling was a great game. Padraig enjoyed watching the local Hurling games, and secretly hoped that one day his Seamus would be out there on the field with the best of them. Padraig realised that this would most likely, always be a simple fantasy. In order for it to become a reality, Seamus would need the freedom, to go out and play, and practise Hurley.

Padraig like any other father, had wanted the best for his children, and at one time would have been able to help them achieve, but now he's a broken man. A man who puts his bottle of stout, before everything else in his life. His view of life, for his children, is clouded and tarnished.

"Hello Grandma, said the little ones"

They leaped up excitedly from their seats, and ran towards me for a hug.

" We've been helping Mammy make bread and churn the butter for tonight's dinner."

The children's excited squeals woke their father. Suddenly, you could hear a pin drop. Those poor kids, you could almost read their minds as their father got up from his chair and began walking towards them, at the same time removing the leather belt from his trousers.

" Sorry Daddy, we didn't mean to wake you", came in very faint voices. Would you like some more stout, I can get it for you cried Eefie"

Poor Eefie she was too late. The children had two marks each on their legs from the belt. Padraig was angry

"Now, you little blegards , get back to the table and wait there quietly and say your prayers for forgiveness for waking your poor father after his long day at work"

. "But Da",

" Be quiet Seamous"

Padraig growled, as he began to tell me of his day in the bogs, same old story, regurgitated so many times. Padraig had the view point that no one worked as he did, certainly not his wife, sure what did she ever do these days?

Cleaning a house ,cooking dinners, and telling your kids to get up and go to bed is not work, she spends her days doing nothing, in the eyes of her bullying husband. There was no pleasing Padraig where Eileen was concerned. When she was practising medicine he was full of jealousy. Now she's not able to, she does nothing. Poor Eileen she can't win.

Digging turf was very hard work, if you're to believe a word that comes from Padraig O Shaunesseys mouth. Poor Padraig, he thought that he had such a hard life. Out in the bogs in the glorious sunshine, listening to nature all day long, never a thought for Eileen, who had so lovingly prepared his breakfast of eggs, collected fresh from the nest, that morning, and bacon, which she sliced from the half side of pig hanging in the outhouse and sandwiches carefully wrapped to keep fresh for his lunch. Eileen's a dedicated wife to the man she once loved, but now, surely just tolerates for the sake of her children, the sake of her family. A very poor reason, a wrong reason to stay in a drunken violent marriage. Eileen has on many an occasion, seen the way in which Eamon O Hara looks at her. She can see the longing in his eyes. She has the same feelings, but for so many varied reasons, cannot act upon them. Eamon enquires with sensitivity, understanding and such compassion, if she is all right?

Her fear of Padraig. Eamons fear of Padraig, combined together, has to be greater than her fear of God, if she were to look outside of her marriage. Father John, on many an occasion had told Eileen.

"We all have our cross to bear Eileen; you will get your reward in heaven "

Eileen knew how to settle her husband down. She spoke to him with a very soothing and gentle tone.

"Padraig You sit down there and save your energy, rest your weary legs."

Padraig slouched backwards in his chair. Minutes later the noise had begun again. Seamus had a quiver in his almost whispering voice. He sorta struggled to get the words out.

"Jesus mammy he's asleep already"

No risk was to be taken of disturbing the brute again. Eileen knew her husband like the back of her hand. She knew that a little sympathy from her would keep him content, well for a while anyhow. Eileen's hope was that she, the children, her mother and their guests, could try to enjoy a pleasant evening. That hope was dashed faster that she would want it to be. No more than what seemed like five minutes, but in reality was probably half an hour, it all began again. Padraig suddenly shouted out, leaping from his chair at the same time.

"Oh be Jaysus Eileen, I swear, I swear I just saw a ghost"

The two youngest children ran towards their mother, wrapping themselves round her legs, the colour drained from their faces. Eefie started to cry. That was a scene that occurred in the house on many, many occasions. Seamus stood up, he breathed a very heavy sigh, he looked calm and dignified with a maturity way beyond his years. He felt like he had enough. He wasn't going to take another outburst from his father. The family were not going to endure his brutality any longer. Seamus decided that he would tell it as it is, and if Padraig didn't like it then well that would have to be his problem. Seamus spoke to his father, with the calm power of reasoning. Something that Padraig didn't know anything about, didn't understand.

"Well Da if you did see a ghost, then maybe it's what you deserve; now you see how it feels to be frightened. That's the way you make other people feel all the time. Well me Ma and the girls anyway. You don't frighten me I can defend me self".

Padraig was standing still, as if frozen to the spot. He had a blank look, yet a look of terror on his face. I was thinking how proud I felt of my grandson, how grown up he had behaved, and the way that he had stood up to his drunken father using the power of words, instead of the power of fists. Padraig looked at his son in silence, and then walked outside to the meadow. Seamus followed his father. They both walked over to the old house. I hadn't seen Padraig over there for a very long time. Did he really see a ghost? Was it John, is that why he has gone to Johns favourite place. Father and son went round to the back where Johns chair sits. I saw Padraig bless himself, making the sign of the cross on his forehead. Seamus got on bended knees

"Come on Da pray with me"

He encouraged his father. Later Seamus told me, that he had thought, that if his father prayed at Johns chair, then John might help him, to stop drinking, and to allow his children to experience the life they deserved.

Eileen swept her long red hair back into a pony tail. Her elegant body, slightly tanned, went some way to disguise the bruising on her arms. I knew that Padraig was hurting my daughter, however, she would never admit to it. It was almost, as though she thought, that if she denied his abuse, he might stop. A loose floorboard on the stairs, I was told, was responsible for many a trip which resulted in Eileen breaking a rib, or sustaining heavy bruising from her many falls down the stairs.

" Is my skirt too tight she wondered "?

 Eileen, with her self esteem sweeping the floor, had no idea what a beautiful woman she was. Her academic achievements are seemingly now wasted. Padraig and his lifestyle have brought so much pressure to bear on my daughter that she no longer has the will, the confidence, the enthusiasm or the time really, to go out there like she used to, and teach the future of this, and surrounding villages, the skills required to attain whatever it might be that they hope to achieve in life. An education that would give them a better life than the one she watched her family experience. Getting up at 5am to milk the cows, and still in the cows barn at 10pm, is something that her parents and grandparents all did. Education in the academic sense was never a priority in their lives. "It's all in the slow lane" was an expression that she many times heard her father say.

Eileen had gone through a great struggle to get her professional career. She had hoped to encourage many more Irish farming women to do the same. She could no longer see the possibility of all this. She seemed to have lost what she needed, in order to be the person who could go out there, and do those things. The change in Eileen was totally due to her blegarding tyrant of a husband of many years, from a shotgun wedding, never paying her a compliment, constantly putting her down, psychically and emotionally abusing her. Padraig when under the influence, which he regularly was these days, would reduce his wife to tears with his words of poison. He would carry on, as though he had played no part in the first conception

"You're a tart Eileen he would scream at his wife"

This happened on more than one occasion. Padraig would have no remorse for his outbursts. He would then tell her, that it was her tarty behaviour that caused them to be punished by God, in the drowning of their first born child Martin. Padraig was relentless in those outbursts. I almost believe that when he was in a drunken stupor, that he actually believed his accusations. Eileen too, had suffered untold sorrow from the death of their first born. You could see it in her brow. She had made many huge efforts to overcome the tragedy, and to a large extent, she had been successful in doing that. She had been to the holy shrine of Lourdes in France, together with Padraig, where they prayed for a greater understanding of why their son had drowned. Eileen was a great believer in that things always happen for a reason. She felt, that if herself and Padraig could feel that they knew why they had to lose Martin, it would help with the recovery process. Eileen did get some truly amazing strength from her visit to Lourdes. Padraig choose to reject any feelings of comfort, and continued with his life of self pity, and alcohol indulgence.

Seamus Leaves

The morning arrived. Eileen's heart ached. She would not let her son see how she was feeling. She knew that he had to do this; he had to make a life for himself away from his bullying father. It was a nice morning and almost the end of summer. She was up at 5am. She would have some quiet time before the family got going and all the chaos which that might create. Eileen went for a walk to the river. The sound of the running water always seemed to have a calming effect. She sat on the embankment thinking about her family and how it was beginning to fall apart. She watched the ripples that were created, when a tiny fish moved around by the stones. Eileen wondered what was going to happen to the O Shaunesseys and in particular if her husband might ever acknowledge how he lives his life and controls the life's of his children and of herself to some extent. The hour went quickly. She saw Kathy walking over the hill. Kathy was helping out with the milking this morning. The girls hugged each other then walked slowly back to Eileen's. Seamus and Eefie were already up

"Jaysus mammy, times getting on, where have you been"

Seamus had an edge in his voice. Eileen wondered how her son was feeling. She decided not to ask. The smell of frying bacon was very appetising. Seamus had a good breakfast. The train was leaving at eleven am. The car arrived at half past nine. Eefie was crying. The girls refused to go to school. Eileen decided to accept their decision, as they needed to see their brother onto the train

"God knows when he will come home mammy, we have to do this. We have to be sure that our brother gets on that train and to see it with our own eyes"

Tears were welling up in Eefies eyes again. She had tried so very hard to be brave. Her sister took her outside. She couldn't upset Seamus, on the day that he was leaving for England, for London and the bright lights. Padraig had gone into the fields. It was almost as though he would be in denial of his son's departure. Seamus was more the man. He shouted to his father that it was time to leave. Padraig was grumbling to himself. Seamus decided that it was best left. That there would be no goodbyes between him and his father. The journey to Ballaghaderreen seemed to take forever Seamus boarded the train to Dublin. It brought back memories for Eileen of her own young days. She wondered if he would choose an empty carriage like she used to. He didn't. He shared with two other young men who looked as though they should still be at school. There were no improvements in the train condition. The windows were still dirty the seats with torn cloth on the backs. Eileen wondered if maybe it was actually the very same locomotive that she had sat in all those years ago. The train sat for ten minutes before chugging out of the station. The girls and their mother waved Seamus off. As it pulled away, Seamus had his face leaning against the dirty window. He was furiously waving back at his family. For a moment, tears ran down the faces of all of them.   Eileen then made the decision that she had to be strong for her own sake as well as that of her daughters.

"Come on you two, this isn't good enough. Eileen spoke to her daughters in a stern but caring tone. We need to understand that Seamus is going to have a better life, and be Jaysus, it won't be long, before he comes back to the village, telling us all the craic from London".

The girls smiled. They left the railway station and walked down to the square, where they had a sandwich and coffee in Donovan's bar, then set out on the long journey home. Eefie protested a little, saying that she was tired and her legs were hurting, and any other excuse she could think of, in order to get out of a five mile walk home. When things were especially tense, Eileen would take her children on a long walk.

" Sure the exercise and fresh air will clear away the cobwebs she told them."

Eventually they would stop protesting. This was one of those days. Padraig didn't go with his family. He grumbled he groaned about anything and nothing. He made every excuse possible for not going to the train. Maybe it had been his way of avoiding a farewell to the child he knew he had driven away.

"Sure I'm not well Eileen and anyway he doesn't want me there. Seamus doesn't want me there, he hates me"

This was becoming fairly common place for padraig. As he often did, Padraig was once again welling in self pity. Forever playing the victim when in fact he is usually the perpetrator. Taking no responsibility for his own actions. No responsibility for the fact, that he had driven our eldest grandchild away, and I'm in no doubt that he will drive his daughters away also. Evening arrived; Annette and Eefie sat by the river. Eileen was angry, she confronted her husband.

" How can you let our son leave and not say a proper goodbye? You're a more selfish man than I realised"

Padraig began to make his excuses, just like he previously did, saying that he was unwell, and that Seamus was better off without him anyhow. That the parting would be easier for their Son if he didn't see his father being upset. That Seamus wouldn't feel guilty for making his parents feel that way.Padraig somehow felt better about himself when he thought that he had convinced Eileen that he cared about them more than his alcohol and his own inner feelings. He had a long way to go before that thought was now going to be realised. Eileen began to fill up with rage. How dare Padraig take that view? She did her deep breathing technique which she had learned in Dublin. Slowly and gradually she calmed herself down. Eileen decided that Padraig was not worth her, making herself so upset. He was always going to be a totally selfish man, and no amount of confrontation or discussion would ever change that. Eileen walked away and began to prepare for bed. She got down on her knees and prayed to the lord, that her Son would have a safe journey to England, and that her daughters would find happiness in their lives. She actually surprised herself, when she found herself praying for Padraig, and asking God to give him some understanding, of the trauma he has put their children through. Eileen would continue to nurture their daughters, and live in the hope that maybe one day, Padraig would wake up, to the reality of the situation he had created.

The Friends

Jackie was preparing for her trip to the States

"The United States of America exclaimed Angie. Oh my God you can't! What about Eamonn? What's he got to say about this and what about the children? Who's taking care of them? Who will push Brendan to school? who will clean his nose when it runs constantly? Who Jackie? who will do those things?"

David came running in "Mammy he cried, Daddy's home."

Jackie told her Son to be quiet, in her very selfish tone.

" Please Angie not a word. I haven't told Eamonn yet, I have to choose my moment".

Jackie knew that Eamon would be annoyed. She was leaving her children again, leaving Eamon to care for them as she had done on a previous occasion. Jackie jumped at the chance when the announcement was made by her boss, that there was an opportunity to go to New York for six months working in a sister company. As usual, Jackie thought only of herself. Her decision was made she would tell her boss.

"I can do it John. I can go and to be sure the break will do me good and do Eamon and the kids good too".

John had to be sure. He needed someone who would not change their mind or have their mind changed for them. He questioned her, about how this move, could ever possibly be good for her husband and for her children. Leaving her husband with two small children, for a second time and one of them being severely disabled. He was astonished at her lack of concern for her family. Jackie was not interested in that side of the argument. She thought only about herself, and the benefits this trip would bring for her. She attempted to persuade John how good it would be for the company, as she was the most experienced member of staff there. That was the truth, she had worked in the company for a lot of years. She knew the ins and outs of it all. She was a true asset to her employer .The decision was finalised. She would leave shortly for America. Jackie felt elated

Eamons a tall, quiet, gentle man with greying hair, a small balding patch on the crown, receding at the front and at such a young age. The stress of being married to Jackie, and having a disabled child has all taken a toll on him. Teaching at the local school is a job he loves. It gives him an escape, somewhere to hide away when it's all too much, and of course it gives him lots of free time to be with his family in the long summer holidays.

Eamon and Jackie were lovers at the tender age of 15. They had lived in adjoining villages and attended the same National school. That of course was the only school for miles and miles. Eamons family were full of concern. The night they saw him walking home from the river with Jackie felt like one of the worst nights of their lives'. This they decided was something that had to stop and had to stop immediately. They tried to persuade him not to get involved. They considered Jackie to be a very unsuitable friend for their Son. Eamon would go places in life, but not if she's in the background. They sent him to Sligo for six months.

"Your Uncle Johnnie needs some help on the land."

They had hoped, that Jackie, being the sort she was, would have found another boyfriend by the time Eamon returned back home. She did show a keen interest in some local lads. There was a band playing at the clubhouse. Eamons parents could be quite manipulating. They bought a ticket for Jackie .

"You have a nice time enjoy yourself, sure Eamon will be delighted that you went".

Oh my god Mrs O Hara, that's so generous of you. Sure I will have a great time, and there's Eamon stuck at his Uncles in Sligo. Eamons mammy was desperate to get Jackie away from her son. She could see that Jackie would never be a good wife or girlfriend even, for any man. Isn't it funny how as parents we can see those traits when our children never can? She was determined to save her son from a messed up life. Jackie was not impressed by the boys at the clubhouse.

Mrs O Hara tried to hide her disappointment, when Jackie told her, that there wasn't anyone she was interested in, at the dance. The six months went by quickly. Eamons Uncle didn't need him anymore. Eamon left his Uncles home in Sligo. He decided that teaching was what he wanted to do with his life. He went to College in Balla. That's where he trained, to become an every subject teacher, in the hope that one day he would get a job in the local National School. Jackie attended the same college, in order to pursue business studies, and in particular to develop her interest, in the selling of land and houses. Within a short period of time Eamon and Jackie had resumed their relationship. They would sometimes sit together, on the college wall at lunch times in the sunshine. They often spoke about, how her parents, were delighted about their relationship, and his parents wanted them apart. Jackie had heard them talking to their son on more than one occasion

"Jaysus Eamon why don't you open your eyes, she's no good she will ruin your life "

For a lot of people, hearing those words would have been enough to make you decide that an end was in sight. Not for Jackie though. This, in some ways, seemed to strengthen her resolve. Jackie wasn't the sort that would be told what to do. She was wild; her parents knew she was wild. They were happy with the relationship. They considered Eamon to be such a nice quiet gentle man. He would be a good influence for Jackie, he will calm her down. He will help her to see, that one day, she will want to have her own family. Jackie constantly had wandering eyes, and loved to swing it about with the other lads at College.

" It's just a laugh Eamon, I'm not hurting anyone"

It was hurting someone, it was hurting her boyfriend. He had often wondered that if he married her, and they had children together, might it calm her down. It was Christmas time. The college had organised a bus, to take the students, to the dance in Charlestown as a special reward for the year's hard work. Eamon and Jackie both went to the dance. Jackie was carrying on in her usual manner. She left Eamon whilst she danced the eight set reel, and then she went outside. Eamon felt frustration building up inside him. He decided that once and for all, he would confront his girl friend. He followed her into the street. Before he got chance to speak, Jackie announced

"Jaysus Eamon I know that I've treated you bad. I'm ashamed of myself"

Eamon was surprised. This was happening easier than he thought it might be. Jackie had never in the past admitted to being in the wrong. She had tears in her eyes. Eamons desire for confrontation disappeared. He pulled her close

"Shh Jackie don't cry it's not that bad".

Oh my god how wrong he was. Eamon there's something I need to tell you. She became stern faced again. She was cold in her tone with no regard for how her imminent news might make him feel. Eamon I'm pregnant, I'm seven weeks gone, and yes I know, it couldn't possibly be yours, as we have never, well you know. She tried to make excuses for herself. God Dam it I've wanted you Eamon. I've wanted to go behind the barns with you, when I visit at your parents place. I've wanted to take you to my bed when my parents have been out. Jaysus Eamon I love you, I'm a woman with needs, with desires. You're never interested, you're always telling me

"But we are Catholics Jackie, there's no sex out of wedlock".

Well this is the price to pay, for your holy, Catholic rules .The colour drained from Eamons face, he stumbled backwards almost falling. The woman he was in love with was having another man's baby. They stood in silence for what seemed like an eternity. Eventually Eamon spoke.

"How could you Jackie. I know that you like a good time, I didn't know that you are a tramp "

Eamon immediately retracted his words which had been spoken in anger. This is the woman he loves and has been in love with for such a long time now.

Jackie admitted once again, that she had behaved badly. She made a promise to her boyfriend. I've made a decision. I'm going to England .I'm going to have the baby, then have it adopted. I will tell people, that I need to see a bit of the world. No one will ever find out about the baby. Will you give me another chance? Eamon took some time to think. He decided that everyone should be given a second chance in life. He hugged her, they went back inside. Eamon went to the stage alone. He spoke to the band. Later that evening an announcement was made.

"Would Eamon O Hara, and his girl friend Jackie, come to the front of the hall please"

Jackie began to tremble. What had Eamon done, was he going to embarrass her by telling everyone about the way she had abused their relationship. I can't go up there she protested. In his usual gentle manner he took hold of her hand

" Come on Jackie it's all right"

They moved forward together. There was a deadly silence in the room; you could have heard a pin drop. To Jackie's amazement Eamon got down on one knee. He made a proposal of marriage. Jackie fainted; the shock was all too much for her, and after what she had told him that evening about the pregnancy she simply couldn't believe what was happening. Ten minutes later she was sitting upright with cold water being sponged on her forehead. She agreed to marry Eamon. The room went up in laughter and cheers. She and Eamon left the dance early that night. They walked the long journey home. It was time to clear their heads, and think about, how soon they could put a plan in place for the trip to England, or should she keep the baby, and say that it is his. If she had it adopted, would they go to England together, or would Jackie go on her own? So many options for them, so much to think about and plan. They had to make a hasty decision if adoption was the plan. Jackie had no maternal feelings at all at this point. She wasn't about to have her life ruined, by a screaming, pee, and poo making machine. Yes that's how Jackie thought of babies. She was pushing Padraig to accept her original decision, and he knew that he would have to.

How, and when, they would tell their parents that at least Jackie was leaving. Eventually they decided to leave together, so that Eamon could help her get settled. Help her find a place to live, where they took in women like her. A small gathering of both families was planned at Jackie's parent's home. The double announcement was made. Eamons mammy protested, till she couldn't protest any more. She eventually realised, that no matter what she said, or done, those two were going to get married. Jackie's parents were delighted with the news, that Eamon O Hara was taking their wild daughter on a four week tour of England, and then going to make her his wife. Their daughter would at last settle down. Their life's couldn't get any better at that moment. The O Haras were a lot less pleased. The news of the baby, would remain a secret, between Eamon and Jackie

The House For Pregnant Girls

Eamon organised, and paid for the sailing. Jackie, to his surprise offered to help out

"Its all right Jackie you'll need your money in England ".

The couple travelled over to Dublin on the bus. They were booked onto the sailing from Dunlahire, on Thursday the 4th January at 6 o clock in the evening. The boat arrived in Holyhead six hours later. Eamon had arranged for them to take a bus from Holyhead to a small town in Yorkshire. He had heard through contacts at the church, that there was a house there that looked after pregnant unmarried girls, who wished for their baby to go for adoption. Baby would be taken at birth. There would be no opportunity for bonding. This suited Jackie. The Irish option would not have met her needs. The girls in the Irish homes were treated like slaves. They kept their baby, up to about the age of two years. Breastfeeding, bonding then ultimately separation for adoption. Eamon and Jackie arrived at the house hungry and thirsty. Jackie wasn't as brave as she had considered herself to be. She felt frightened. What if no one liked her, or talked to her? They knocked on the door. A kindly looking woman, with rather a strange accent, answered. Jackie introduced herself. The woman told them that men were not allowed inside the house. She told them where they could find food and a bed for Eamon for the night. Four weeks later, Eamon returned back home, to take up his studies again. He told everyone that Jackie liked England so much, that she decided to stay there for a while, and would rejoin her studies class at the beginning of the following year. He gave an envelope to her parents. It contained a letter, saying how sorry she was for all her misgivings. She hoped that they would forgive her, and she would see them on her return. Jackie got herself a job at the local shop. The money wasn't good but every little helped. She knew that she had to save for her ticket to sail back to Ireland when everything was over with and she felt well enough. Three weeks after Eamon returned back to Ireland, there was a telegram in his name. It was from Jackie. The message was brief and simple. She had taken the precaution of insuring that no one, except Eamon, got a clue from the telegram

"Stuff has happened I'm coming home next week".

Eamon breathed a sigh of relief. He figured that nature had intervened. This surely had to be the best solution in the circumstance. On her return, Jackie confirmed his thoughts. There was no known reason, it simply happened. The lady at the house had called the doctor. Rest was all she could do. It wasn't enough. Everyone at the house had been supportive and reassuring Jackie in the thought that she would be feeling distraught at her loss. They clearly didn't know her very well. Eamon was glad to have her home. Jackie could tell lies easily. It was no problem for her to tell people that she simply decided that she didn't like the English way of life after all, and anyway she was missing her boyfriend. The following months were a little tense. Jackie would often have outbursts, declaring that she wished to have her old life back and of her uncertainty of her love for the man who was to be the brick in her life. Eamon wouldn't be defeated he wanted this woman .They were married two years later. It was an Easter wedding. Eamon was up at seven. He needed to be sure that the house was as clean as it could be before he brought his bride back there. His parents and in particular his mother made a last minute attempt to change his mind about the wedding.

"Sure it's not too late Eamon and you would be doing Jackie a favour. You must see that she will never really settle down, she's not the sort who would".

His mothers tone was desperate. She could see the mistake in what he was doing; see how his life would be, with Jackie as his wife. Eamon wasn't hearing a word of it. Eamon had been saving up very hard. He had bought a very smart dark blue suit, white shirt, and pale blue tie. It was time for him to get dressed. The car arrived from Balla.

" Hurry up ma there's not much time left".

The O Hara family travelled together in almost silence. The car arrived at the chapel, ten minutes before the service was due to begin. Eamon paced up and down the car park before going into the chapel. His bride to be arrived. He thought how beautiful she looked. She had been given a white dress by her parents. The priest began. Mrs O Hara was waiting for an opportunity in the service to raise her objections against the marriage. The chapel was packed out. The doors were closed. It was hot inside the chapel. Mrs O Hara was overcome by the heat. She was taken outside for air, just at the right moment to stop her embarrassing her son. On her return the service had completed. Her Son was now a married man. There was nothing she could do. She decided that she would try to change her view of Jackie as this would be more supportive to Eamon. It all seems like a very long time ago now. Jackie and Eamon went on to have two children

Jackie loved the bright lights, the whispers when she entered a room. The feeling of being the centre of attention as she usually was, whilst in her parents' home. She tried to create this attention to herself wherever she went. She would usually succeed, either by her wild behaviour, or her outlandish dress sense. Jackie had been working in the Estate Agents in town for about four years. Her position there was an important one. Although the financial gain wasn't immense, the gain to her self confidence was absolutely huge. The thought of her trip to the states sent shivers down her spine. Oh yes, Jackie loved herself more than anyone else.

Brendan and David are adorable children.Brendans the eldest almost 11, David's almost 9 but in many ways much older than his brother. Brendan, sadly for him, has a disability. There are no facilities for disabled children or adults for that matter.

"Jaysus Eamon, he should never have been born. Our lives are destroyed, and look at him; he doesn't have a life, not a real life".

These are words that he has heard more times than he cares to remember. Jackie had a sharp tongue, a callous mind where her child was concerned. Eamon was at a loss as to how to deal with his wife's outbursts. He's already done all the appealing to her better nature many times in the past. It's never made a difference. On one of her trips to America Jackie was fortunate enough to discover a rich Aunt. The amazement of Jackie simply chatting to a lady at the office one day, and making the discovery that she knew a long lost relative. The Irish community was strong in New York. Everybody knew everybody else's business. Jackie wondered how she could approach her Aunt. Would the shock of her simply landing on the doorstep be too much? Should she write first, or call her on the telephone? She in her usual selfish manner, put her own needs above those of her aunt, and simply arrived at the door. The house was grand with a large garden in the suburbs of New York. Oh be jaysus, you should see the size of it. There must be at least six bedrooms. Jackie took a deep breath; she knocked loudly on the wooden door. A middle aged lady appeared at the door. Although her hair was greying there was a striking appearance which reminded Jackie of her Grandmother. She spoke with an American accent which had a tinge of Irish brogue. Jackie stood there speechless. Her Aunt wasn't sure who her visitor was. Jackie introduced herself. The ladies shook hands, and then Kathleen leaned forward to hug her niece. It was not reciprocated. Kathleen would soon discover that her niece lacked emotion. Jackie had a surge of jealousy

"Jaysus Aunt Kathleen, you've done well for yourself. How long have you been living here? Where's your husband? How many kids do you have? Any Grandchildren yet?"

Jackie had so many questions for her Aunt. The Aunt invited Jackie to stay over for the weekend. Kathleen had to wipe the tears away as she listened to her Niece. Thoughts of her deceased mother and father (Jackie's Grandmother and Grandfather) came into her mind. No one had told Kathleen about the accident or the fact that both her parents had suddenly died. The burial had taken place more than five years before she found out.

"At least they went together Jackie".

Kathleen began to talk about this with her niece, in a sensitive manner. She assumed that Jackie would be upset by the discussion. She was wrong. She didn't know her niece at all, and to assume that she had her mother's caring, unselfish nature was certainly the wrong assumption to have made. The driver was drunk, and you know that they never travelled in a car, but, that trip to Dublin was different, and then will you look at what happened. Kathleen waited for a response from her niece. Jackie wasn't interested in what her Aunt had been saying about her grandparents.

"Mammy's talked about you loads but never really seemed to know where you lived or what your life is like.Jaysus don't you ever want to come back to the old place".

Kathleen was hesitant in her response.

" It might be nice Jackie, maybe one day, but for now, I have my life and my family here in America"

The two ladies enjoyed each other's company, so many stories to tell. Kathleen shared about her voyage over the ocean many years ago and how she met a young and handsome American boy. How her parents didn't want her to leave Ireland. How she had wanted a better life for herself and didn't want to stay and marry some farmer or other. How she had worked as a seamstress to earn the money for her voyage. Eventually her parents relented and at the age of nineteen she had set sail to America. How she can't even begin to imagine what the home place might look like now. How she wished that she had returned to the homestead before the death of her parents. Kathleen longed to see them once more, she could make them understand how her leaving was truly the best thing that she could ever have done. How her American boy became her husband, and then qualified as a doctor. He now specialises in spina bifida. Oh how she regrets not having been in constant touch with her Irish family, and not having them share a little of her good luck and fortune. Jackie allowed her Aunt to reminisce, but didn't really pay much interest to anything that she was saying, other than the fact that she could see that Kathleen now has a wealthy lifestyle. Jackie wondered how she could cash in on it a little or maybe a lot even.

Jackie went on, and on, about her life in Ireland. She told her Aunt to listen carefully and by doing so the Aunt would see how unfortunate Jackie is, by comparison to Kathleen. She wanted her Aunt to pity her. You remember the O Haras, but which ones Kathleen wondered. There were lots of O Hara families round our way

"I've married Eamon O Hara and we have nothing"

Jackie's mind was full of resentment. Why had she married Eamon O Hara? Did she once upon a time fall in love with him? Had she married someone else then maybe she wouldn't have had a disabled child! Maybe she would be living in a nice house like Padraig and Eileen are. Maybe that she would have a happy life. Oh it was so easy to blame Eamon for everything that's wrong in her life. Jackie would never take responsibility for herself. Living in a thatched farm house, which isn't much more than a barn, with a concrete floor, and no nice furnishings, and into the bargain, if our life's weren't bad enough, he decided to send us a disabled child. Her tone was bitter; the words came with a sting. Aunt Kathleen struggled to understand her niece. How could she speak this way about her child? Her own flesh and blood.

"Surely he's a blessing Jackie .God always does those things for a reason"

Aunt Kathleen was getting to know the sort of person her niece is. Jackie, a beautiful woman on the outside. She was tall, with long red hair full of curls, and a pretty smile. She was perfection to look at, but underneath that beautiful exterior, she was cold, callous and uncaring. She wanted nice things; she was materialistic as well as selfish. Jackie sat down beside her aunt. She told her about the problems that Brendan has and how he can't walk. She didn't say anything nice or caring or positive about him. She didn't mention her other son at all. She told Kathleen about how the tears pour down Eamons face when he looks at his child lying helplessly in his bed or on the cold floor. Kathleen was by now getting a good picture of the sort of man that Jackie was married to. She sensed that he was very caring and must be tolerant to put up with her Niece.

" You can lack compassion a little Jackie".

She had not made a very good impression on her Aunt. Jackie didn't have any tears, didn't show any emotion but then this was typical of her. She was a cold self centred woman, who always put herself and her own needs in front of everyone else's. Aunt Kathleen was compassionate. She had been raised in a loving caring family. Her husband's family were kind and caring and above all, very generous. It was second nature to Kathleen to be that way too. She was a wealthy woman who looked on the less fortunate through caring eyes.

"I will help you Jackie. I will do whatever I can".

Jackie's eyes lit up. She spoke to her aunt, without taking a breath.

"Oh my god aunt Kathleen, thank you. Are we hitting the shops in New York tomorrow? I could use some new clothes for work, and a pair of those shoes with the pointed toes. You know the ones I mean they're the latest in the shops."

."No Jackie, I don't mean help you, for you. For once can't you be a little selfless and maybe think about your poor disabled child because that's who I'm thinking of. I've got visions of Brendan in the wheel chair".

Jackie was flabbergasted. Her Aunt had stood up to her, put her in her place so to speak. Jackie who was used to getting her own selfish way for once had fallen flat. She had met her match in her Aunt Kathleen in many ways.

"We will go tomorrow. I will talk to the manufacturers and Brendan will have the best that there is available".

"But Aunt Kathleen, the shoes"

Jackie tried to manipulate her Aunt, It didn't work. Kathleen decided that she wouldn't allow her niece to see her frustration, her anger. She would remain composed and simply tell her

" No Jackie not the shoes. Forget the shoes. We will sort a chair for your little boy".

Kathleen got up early the next morning. She decided she would be generous to her Niece. The compassion might rub off. She brought Jackie a cup of tea in bed. The ladies got ready and left for the city. Jackie was in awe of everything around her. They had a short but brisk walk in a park before they settled down with the manager of the local resources centre. Tell me about your child. The more information I have, the better I can match him to a chair. Jackie was irritated by the amount of questions being asked about her child. She wondered if they could just get on with it quickly. Kathleen finalised the arrangements of the purchase and delivery of a wheelchair from America

."Its done Jackie I've sorted the chair".

Jackie wasn't really listening. Her thoughts were focused on the fact that very shortly she would be leaving her Aunt's house, leaving America. She would be returning to a life that she wasn't overly keen on.

"Are you listening Jackie," her Aunt snapped, she was finding it increasingly difficult to tolerate the selfishness of her sisters daughter. You should try to concentrate a little less on yourself, and a little more on your family, and your children in particular. You just may find some happiness in that way of thinking!"

Jackie didn't accept her Aunts advice. The following morning, Kathleen organised a car to take Jackie to the docks. She waved goodbye to her Aunt. Kathleen wondered if she saw a flicker of emotion.

"Aunt Kathleen it was nice meeting you".

The car drove away from the house, Jackie cried a silent tear. No, it wasn't for the fact that she was saying goodbye to the Aunt she had only just met. Typical of Jackie it was because she didn't get the shoes she had hoped for, in fact, she didn't get any shopping at all for herself. Her Aunt made her mind up and there was no changing it. Jackie needed to learn a lesson, that sometimes it's others first. Kathleen was surprised that her mother hadn't taught her this. Perhaps this weekend might have taught her something at least Kathleen hoped it would have.

Three months into the future and Brendan's life was about to improve. The chair would be shipped across to Ireland, and then transferred by train from Dublin. Jackie and Eamon could collect it from the train station. The Mulligan's lad would then drive them to the house. The plan was in place and what a plan it was. Kathleen felt good about what she had done! The like had never been seen in our village. A child in a wheelchair was unheard of. Brendan would now be able to attend the local school as well as go out to other places. Kathleen had also been in contact with a shop in the town near where Jackie lived with her family. An order of clothing had been placed for the children. They would be the best dressed children the village had ever seen. It was a Saturday morning. The curlew was up early singing his heart out. Eamon got the children up at seven. He wanted to have all the chores out of the way before his wife arrived. He had worked hard keeping the children amused and happy in the absence of their mother. A teacher from another area had stood in at the school on a part time basis. She was home caring for her family. She understood Eamons dilemma and agreed to work three days per week so that he could stay home.

The car came up the borreen. We saw Jackie get out. With arms outstretched Eamon walked over to greet her

"Your home Jackie, how was America. God we missed you, the children missed you. I missed you"

Jackie wasn't very responsive. She offered her bags to Eamon to carry for her. She did not reciprecate his show of emotion and delight to be in his company once again.

"I'm tired. The boat took forever, the sea was rough, the crossing was severe, and then I had to wait for hours for the train from Dublin".

Eamon was feelings a little anxious. He was uncertain about his wife's feelings and wondered why she was being so cold towards him.

"Come and sit down beside me" he whispered to her.

She didn't. She stood in front of Eamon, and asked where the children were. She didn't enquire for their well being. She didn't make any attempt to see them. David was in the bogs with our neighbour gathering some sods of turf. Brendan was on his bed in the top room. His vocal attempts began to get louder. He had heard his mother's voice and I'm confident that he wished to see her. Jackie showed no interest. She told Eamon about the meeting with her rich aunt and about the wheelchair that would be arriving in about two month's time. Eamon was delighted. He could now see a better future for his son, a better future for his family. He had a surge of gratitude for the lady that he hasn't ever met.

"Maybe we will have Kathleen here one day. Wouldn't it be grand if she could meet the children one day?"

Jackie didn't respond for a few minutes. She remained disinterested in her children and her husband. She had an outburst in relation to the possibility of her Aunt coming to visit.

"Be jaysus Eamon you should see how she lives and you want to bring her here, bring her to this dump. No I don't think so, don't you have any shame".

Eamon was disappointed by his wife's reaction and the fact that she considered that her Aunt would be more interested in our home than in our children. Eamon anxiously waited for the arrival of the chair. He was concerned to know that it would be a proper fit for Brendan .Brendan has the innocence of a very young child. He seemed to enjoy his new chair. He laughed uncontrollably when he was put sitting upright, and tried to pull at the straps, that kept him in place. David pushed him, up and down the room, over and over, until he was almost dizzy. David was excited to see his brother being able to get about. The summer holidays were over. Jackie was relieved

" In the name of god Eamon, just push it to school will ya.Just get it out of my sight".

Her harsh words were ringing in the ears of her husband as he attempted to console his other son. Tears were running down David's face

"Why doesn't mammy care about Brendan .Just because he can't talk, or walk, and looks different to all the other children at the school, that's no reason for her to hate him. Why daddy, why?"

Eamon had heard these comments and questions so many times, yet he couldn't find an answer for his son. Eamon, unlike his wife, is a caring compassionate man, who adores both his children and can't begin to imagine why Jackie feels this way about her own flesh and blood. Eamon began the long journey to the school where he worked. God it was hard. Bag full of books, equipment for Brendan. Medication for his epilepsy. Clean nappies for changing. Eamon trying to teach his handicapped son is simply not working. The damage is too severe. Jackie doesn't care. Selfish, callous, uncaring Jackie. As long as she is all right then what else matters.

"Morning sir. Can we look after Brendan today? Can we play with his chair? Can we push it in the playground?"

The children all loved Brendan, his cute smile, even his runny nose which needed constant attention. As the children took control of the wheelchair, Eamon felt an overwhelming sense of relief. At least this was one place where he could have time away from his disabled son in the knowledge that he was being amused and kept happy. David was off to play with Annette and Effie before the days lessons be

The excuse to see Eileen

Eefie grumbled when she was told to get up for school. But I don't feel well mammy. Eileen decided that maybe her daughter had heard the fight and this was her way of staying home to be sure her mother was all right. Eileen would never be manipulated by anyone. Come on Eefie it's a nice morning, the suns shining and your breakfasts ready. The child didn't eat very much. She left for the long walk to the school. She sat in her lesson then suddenly there was a squeal from her desk. She had been uncontrollably sick. Eamon got a bucket, and some water, from the pump in the yard. He cleaned it all up and took Eefie outside for some air. She had developed a rash. It was all over her face by now, and spreading down her neck and arms. The onset was sudden. As she was on the school premises, Eamon told himself that he was responsible. He would take the child home; he couldn't let someone else do this. He borrowed a bicycle from the post office which was built right next to the school and rode back to Eileen's house with Eefie across the front bar. Eefie vomited again on the journey home. Though Eileen no longer practised as a doctor she would always have the knowledge. She would know what was wrong with her daughter. Eamon hadn't been to the Shaunessys home for a long time, hadn't seen Eileen or Padraig for a long time. He had heard the rumours though that Padraig was drinking heavily and sometimes the children would have unexplained marks on their arms. They always said that it happened when they were playing. Eamon walked into the house without announcement

"What are you doing here Eamon? Why is Eefie home? What's wrong with Eefie"?

Eamon was shocked to find Eileen sitting in a corner crying. She had bruises on both her arms and finger marks on her cheek. Eileen was shocked to see Eamon walk through her front door "

Be Jaysus Eileen what's happened to you? What's he done to you? Ill bloody kill him!"

Eamon was angry. He knew that he had to calm himself down. Eamon, usually gentle, gentle Eamon suddenly and probably for the first time in his life began to worry that he couldn't calm himself down. He had to find a diversion from his feelings.

" Oh never mind lets deal with Eefie first and then we can sort you out. She's got the measles I thought that I should bring her home".

Eamon put Eefie to bed like it was the most natural thing in the world for him to do

"Be a good girl for your mammy. You've got the measles and need to stay warm, to bring the rash out completely. Then you will start to feel better".

Eefie settled, and in no time at all she was fast asleep. She liked Eamon. She liked him as a teacher and also as a friend, when he came to visit her parents. Eamon surprised himself. He knew that Eefie had the measles. Why then did he take her home? Why didn't he let someone else do it?. He wrestled with his own thoughts. Was it an excuse to see Eileen? Eamon had been aware of his feelings for a very long time. He knew that he liked Eileen, had a great respect for her, and felt quite sure that she felt the same way. So many times he thought about the possibilities of them being together. He would dream about being in her arms, and holding her in his. He dreamt about making love to her, and knew that even in his wildest dreams, that this is all it could ever be. He dreamt about going home from the school every day to be greeted by Eileen and for her to want him as much as he wanted her. So many times he dismissed those thoughts. He knew, that right here in holy Ireland, where everyone watched your every move, and everyone had a saintlier than though attitude, that he could never get together with another man's wife.

"Eamon come and sit by me. Eileen had made some tea, her eyes were dry, not a sniffle in sight. You're a good man Eamon O Hara, you care about people. She was passionate in her tone. You live a decent life, not like that drunken blegard that I'm married too. Be

Jaysus Eamon I'm so unhappy. He's so controlling he's a brute. He's so insular and so selfish. Never considers anyone but himself and always getting drunk and beating me and the children. I'm a trained doctor for god's sake and look at me now an absolute jabbering wreck and all because of him. Eileen shocked herself by her outpouring. Jaysus Eamon I'm sorry I shouldn't go on like that".

As she got up to walk away, she could feel his eyes penetrating on her back. For many a day she had longed to be held in the arms of Eamon O Hara, in the arms of a man that truly cared about her. Eileen knew how much Eamon cared, she wished, and wished, for what she knew could never be. She attempted to get her visitor to leave.

"Goodbye Eamon and thank you for bringing Eefie home it was grand of you, sure I'll see you at mass on Sunday".

Eamon refused to leave.

"I'm not walking away from the woman I love, and leaving her to that blegard, to do more abuse when he sobers up enough to walk in from the top barn. Yes Eileen that's where he is. I saw him when I came up the borreen. He didn't even ask why his child had been brought home from school".

"Jaysus Eamon do ya realise what you've just said. You said that I'm the woman you love, and I love you too".

Eamon couldn't believe what he had just heard.

" What did you say Eileen? Say it again; say it just one more time".

He took her into his arms. They kissed. A long and lingering, passionate kiss They had a long embrace. Eileen felt warmth like she had never felt before. Eamon cried some tears.

"Oh God Eileen how good this feels, but the unfairness of it all. There will never be a way for us, other than to be in secret".

The following weeks and months saw them both have secret meetings. They fell deeper and deeper in love with each other. They both longed to be in each other's arms. Their meetings on one hand, made life more tolerable for them both with their respective partners, on the other hand it made life more intolerable. They wanted a permanency to their relationship; however they both understood that this would never be possible. They talked lots about their respective marriages. They supported each other on an emotional level. After some time Eileen and Eamon made a heart wrenching decision, to stop seeing each other in a romantic way, and to try again to reconcile with their marital partners

The Letter.

Padraig was excited. He could see a figure in the distance coming over the bridge on a bicycle. A few minutes later he was at the front door

."Here's the postman Eileen. There's another letter from Seamus".

Eileen was excited, she had longed to hear from her son and to know how he's doing in London. To know when she can expect to see him and to see if her prayers have been answered. She wished to have Seamus home for Christmas. Padraig tore open the envelope.

"He's busy; he won't be home for Christmas. He's got two bookings over the holiday in that old place in Camden town. Says he's not allowed the time off".

Tears welled up in Eileen's eyes. She knew the truth. And she knew that this was not the truth. She knew that Seamus wasn't too busy to come home. That he had made a choice. Just seventeen and already he didn't want to be with his family, and sure who could blame him. She uttered her words aloud.

"And now Annette's leaving too. She's going to London to be with her brother".

Padraig was shocked

"She can't be she's too young"

"Well she is Padraig, she has a booking on the boat from Dunlaighre on the 2nd January. She wanted to go before Christmas. I persuaded her to stay. You don't know anything about our family anymore".

Eileen was getting angry now and why shouldn't she. She screamed the words at her husband.

"You're just a drunk who doesn't know the day of the week from time to time".

Eileen's body began to tremble, tears now pouring down her face. No comfort from her husband, she struggled to regain her composure. Padraig remained silent, he looked disappointed, but at the same time he had a very serious look on his face.

Padraigs Acknowledgement

Her husband decided that he would take responsibility. He knew in his heart that his wife was right about the reason why their son was staying away and now their daughters leaving too.

" Be jaysus Eileen sure It's me he doesn't want to see, doesn't want to be around, not the family, and Jaysus can you blame the lad. Look what I've turned into. Seamus has sent us fifteen shillings for Christmas. He said we should go to town and get that bench that you were looking at, or five for you, and ten for me to go to Donovan's. I bet that's what he will be thinking. He will be thinking that I will be, as ever, the selfish man who put his stout before everything else in his life. God Eileen he has grown up so much and in a short time too. Living in London has done him good, made him a man".

Padraig made a decision. He knew that he hadn't always been an alcoholic, or an abusive husband and father. He remembered the good times. He would be that person again.

" I will do it Eileen. I will give up the drink. I can do it. I will go to Knock shrine and pray to our lady for help. I will make you proud of me and make the children proud of me".

Should Eileen believe her husband? She has heard those promises before. Did she care? Now one of her children has gone, and soon Annette and Eefie will probably be leaving too. Eileen no longer loved Padraig. How could she, after everything that he has put her through, put their children through? She felt pity and sympathy for her husband but nothing else. Padraig found the road without alcohol very long and lonely. The tremors were worse than he could have ever imagined. He asked Eileen for help and support. She was unsure!

"I'm going in the barn behind the hay shed. I'm taking food and water for three days. Will you lock me in Eileen? Just enough time for the hallucinations to disappear, then I should be on the mend".

Eileen had seen it all before. She knew that three days of punishment wouldn't sort out what had been a problem for the best part of twenty years. She agreed to help. Padraigs screams could be heard throughout the village. There was no other way. No tablet to swallow to make you better. No counselling in our part of the country. It was very hard for Eileen to ignore. The three days seemed like a lifetime to him. If padraig thought that this was the problem resolved then he should have thought again. After two weeks the spiders would still appear crawling over his body from time to time. The mice in their dozens running round in the corner of his bedroom. Eileen was helpless. All she could do was try to reassure him that it wasn't real, but of course, at the point of this happening, he wouldn't hear that.

Padraig however still had his determination to succeed. He would remember how his children have left. How Seamus didn't come home for Christmas. How he beat them and how he abused his wife.

" I will do it Eileen. I will beat this drink thing"

Padraig was full of remorse. Eileen was uncertain if she saw a tear in his eye? On his better days he would try to go back to Knock. The journey was long. Padraig was a good cyclist and of course he loved the scenery along the way. After the visits to Knock Padraig would feel rejuvenated. He felt that he could take the world on, and deal with anything put before him.

Disappointed By Her Husband

After one of his journeys to Knock Padraig was feeling particularly well and in control. He decided to go to the river. He had not been there to go fishing since the day his son had died. As he walked through the meadow, his thoughts were focused on putting the past behind him. He remembered his children and Seamus in particular. He remembered how Seamus had protested the unfairness of it all, and how he had said that their parents and Padraig in particular was suffocating them. Suddenly, as if it happened yesterday, the past flashed in front of Padraig. It was all too much for him. He could see his small child lying helplessly in the stream as if it were the day it all happened. He ran home like a child. Eileen had already left to go to the town. No comfort, no support, he couldn't cope. His resolve about alcohol had diminished. His thoughts about the children and Seamus not coming home for Christmas were a million miles from his head. He had lost it! Eileen had taken the bicycle. The journey to Donovan's was a tedious one. Padraig hadn't been on such a long walk for months and months in fact probably years. He almost collapsed from exhaustion and anxiety as he entered the bar. Jimmy tried to persuade him to leave.

"I will drive you back home Padraig. Take a coffee and then I will get the car out"

Jimmy tried to remind him how well he had done. He took hold of Padraig by his shoulders and faced him directly. He wanted to shake him but knew that wouldn't be helpful. He attempted to find out what had happened to make Padraig come back into his pub. Padraig was silent and wasn't going to change that. He wasn't going to tell Jimmy about the walk to the river! Jimmy continued in his efforts to persuade him to leave

"It's been a few months now Padraig. Don't go down that road again.

Padraig was starting to get frustrated. He was getting angry.

" Just give me the stout will you he screamed. Jaysus that's better ".

Eileen laden with food bags walked passed Donovan's. "I knew it, she murmured to herself." Oh my god I knew it. I knew that he couldn't keep it up. So many empty promises. So much for putting his children before himself. The stupid, stupid man, didn't god give him a brain?"

Eileen was angry, angrier than she had felt in a very long time.

From the corner of his eye Jimmy Donavan saw her peeking through the half glass door.

" Dr O Shaunessey"

Eileen heard Jimmy call out to her. She hadn't been referred to as Dr for such a long long time. It made her feel good. Maybe this was the good that would come from Padraig being in there. Eileen tried to console herself. She decided that she wouldn't confront her husband. She didn't want a scene in public. She told herself, that, this has to be Padraigs decision, and all the nagging in the world won't make any difference. Eileen went home and carried on with her life. No compassion from her now, just a coldness that even she struggled to understand. Eileen was a warm loving caring person. Had Padraig beaten it all out of her she wondered.

 Padraig propped up the bar at Donavan's most days of the week for the following six to seven weeks. Eileen's anger turned to feelings of despair. She had hoped that Padraig becoming dry would have been enough encouragement to bring her son back home. Now it would probably never happen. Eileen was regaining some of the determination, some of the courage that she once had as a young girl. It was Sunday morning. Padraig and Eileen had been to mass together. This was the first time they went out together for a very long time. Eeefie had gone blackberry picking for the day. Eileen prepared dinner. The usual bacon and cabbage with potatoes freshly dug.

"Padraig come and sit beside me I have to tell you something".

A half drunken half sober Padraig staggered to the wooden bench where she sat.

"Listen to me Padraig"

Eileen had a quiver in her voice, she was anxious about what she was going to say to her husband and how he might react but understood that she didn't really have a choice. Eileen began to speak. She reminded her husband of the promises he had made. Of how their children had left because of his behaviours. The worst was yet to come. Eileen for once in her life would put herself before her drunken husband.

"I've had enough Padraig. I'm a doctor I can't even work because of you. Eeefie I'm sure will be leaving soon and then what do I do? Stay here and watch you drink yourself into an early grave. Suffer at your brutal hands. ? Eileen really asserted herself. No Padraig I won't. As soon as Eefie has gone then I'm going too. I'm going to London to find our children. To hold them in my arms like I've craved to do for the past months and months. You don't care. You only think about yourself".

The tears began to well up in Padraigs eyes.

"I'm sorry Eileen, so sorry. I know that I've been a bad husband. I've been a bad father". He begged his wife for one more chance to put things right. One more chance to sort out his drinking problem. Eileen wasn't interested. She heard it so many times and so many times she was let down. "

It's no good Padraig. You say those things when you're in a state of heightened emotion. You never see them through. I've had enough!"

Padraigs mood suddenly changed from remorse to anger.

" You can't go I won't let you go"

He slapped Eileen's face. Eileen slapped him back. Oh my god she shocked herself. Eileen had never raised her hand to anyone in her life let alone to a drunken man who had twice her strength. She then pushed her husband with both hands. He fell backwards onto the concrete floor. Blood was dripping from a small cut to the back of his head.

"Oh get on with it Padraig"

Eileen really didn't care. She walked off to the meadow where she sat for what seemed like an eternity. Padraig eventually sobered up. He thought about the fact that his wife pushed him and caused him injury. This is not her sort of behaviour. What has he driven her too? Padraig had feelings of shame about himself. He realised that Eileen was serious about leaving. He would try again. Sure everybody has one slip up in their lives. Everybody deserves another chance.

The Second Attempt by Padraig

Weeks later, a constantly sober Padraig returned to the river. He sat on the embankment watching the stream trickling slowly. This time he has a new determination. He rethinks the day of Martins death and how he didn't realise his son had followed him. Padraig decided within himself that it wasn't his fault. It was a simple but tragic mistake which anyone could have made. He was going to get rid of the feelings of guilt which he has allowed to destroy his whole family.

" There you are daddy. I've been looking all round for you. It's nice that you're not drinking anymore".

Padraig got up. Suddenly, and right in front of his eyes, was the realisation, the true realisation, that his youngest child was almost a young woman. He was full of remorse.

"Eefie, Jaysus Eefie, I'm so sorry. I'm making this up to you, and to your mammy, Seamus and Annette".

They walked back towards the house together. Padraig held his daughters hand as they went through the meadow. Eefie was feeling excited.She knew what her mammy had been doing all morning. She decided to tell her father in the hope that it might make him feel that Eileen cared for him

" Mammy's been baking again. We can have bread for supper".

Padraig wasn't listening to his child. He had other thoughts and ideas

" Eefie wait. I can do it I want to do it. I want to show you and your mother".

Padraig turned back towards the river.

"Come on Eefie. She wondered what it is that he can do, that he wants to do. Eefie, sit down here beside me and be quiet. They don't come up if there's any noise going on".

She understood. She knew that for the first time since losing her brother, her father was going to do some bare hand fishing again.

" Oh my god Da are you ok. What will mammy say? Will she still leave for London?"

Padraig looked shocked. He wondered how much else his children were aware of that he wasn't. He had a sudden and urgent feeling of intense guilt for all the harm and damage and heartache he had caused and given to his family

"You know about that. When did she tell you? I have to make sure that she doesn't go .I have to get all our lives back to normal".

The lives of the O Shaunessey family are once again in the hands of the reformed alcoholic. Padraig has so much to put right.

Annette Has Left

The train journey to Dublin was the same train that Eileen used all those years ago when she was studying. This time she was at the station saying goodbye to her middle child. The crossing was rough. Dunlaorighe to Holyhead always was rough. Annette couldn't settle. She shared her thoughts with an elderly lady who sat next to her. She told her about her parents and how they lived their lives

"Me da is an alcoholic, always beating us up, hitting me ma I'm going to London to see my brother ".

Annette was tearful when she thought about Eefie left behind .The lady was called Catherine. She was a good listener and showed an interest in what the child was saying.

"Go away with you, does he really hit you, and what about your mammy? Catherine was shocked. Your mammy, an educated lady, a doctor, and lives her life under the abuse of an alcoholic husband and child beater. Shhh child, settle down try to sleep .There's a fair old few miles from Holyhead to London and you look like you haven't had a decent meal in a long time.

The trains don't run very often, I know, I've done it myself enough times, so it will be a long wait when we get there".

Annette was shattered she closed her eyes and the next thing she knew the boat was docking in Holyhead. Catherine was also going to London.

"You stay with me Annette. I can show you where to go ".

Annette felt reassured

." Oh Jaysus that's great. You're older than me; you know what you're doing".

Catherine's wrinkled face told a tale, showed that she had been around a bit. The ladies collected their luggage and walked over the small bridge at the docks. To her astonishment their stood her brother. Eileen had written to Seamus telling him that Annette would be arriving giving all details. She had appealed to her son to look after his sister and to meet her at the docks. The surprises for Annette were the best.

Firstly she's met at the docks by her brother and then this brother who left sleepy Ireland only two years ago has got himself a motorcar. Annette introduced her brother to the kind lady, that she made an acquaintenance with on the boat. As he shook her hand Seamus couldn't help being amazed at the strength of her shake. He felt this demonstrated a degree of sincerity. His father had always told him

"A strong handshake represents a genuine sincere person".

Seamus was relaxing in her company. Catherine accepted the offer, from Seamus, of a lift back to London. It was a long journey from the docks, especially when you've travelled as far as Catherine has and have lived as long as she has. Annette thought that her new friend must be very old. She wondered if she might live for that long. After their meal Annette fell asleep. Catherine explained to Seamus how his sister had shared information about their parents and his family life. She confided in him, that she too, had come from a similar sort of family, and had left Ireland, many, many years ago for the same reasons. Seamus had more than once questioned his own actions. Had he been selfish? Should he have stayed and tried harder to sort things out. Was his mammy all right? Listening to Catherine was very reassuring for him, that he had done the right thing. Catherine was wise. She helped him to understand, that now if he chooses to, he can support his family at a distance, and enjoy freedom for himself at the same time.

Seamus wouldn't hear tell of Catherine paying for the fuel, nor for the meal that the three of them shared. He has come from, what's now a relatively dysfunctional family but that hasn't always been the case. The principles of the O Shauneesseys and the O Haras are still in the genes. It was a long journey from the docks to London. Annette fell asleep.

"Your house is grand Seamus. It's so big, how many people live here?"

Annette was amazed to know that Seamus was sharing the house with some people from County Roscommon. One man he already knew from his flute playing days in O Donovan's... Seamus had arranged for Annette to rent a room in the house next door. It was at the top of the house. A dreary looking room without curtains. Annette decided that she wouldn't be glum about it

"Jaysus Seamus I can easily make some cheap curtains myself. The place will be as bright as me by the time I've done, and you know me, I will be checking up on you all the time. Old mother hen and all that rubbish".

She laughed her infectious laugh. Annette has a bubbly character that lights up a room when she enters. Her presence was nice for her brother. He had missed his family. Now he didn't feel so alone. Seamus felt relaxed in the knowledge that Annette was settling in.Seamus had grown so tall almost six feet.

"Jaysus Seamus have they had you on a stretcher since you left".

Annette was astounded to see how much her brother had changed. How happy he looked. How he was enjoying life in England and especially how he loved working in the Irish club, pulling pints of Guinness, serving bottles of stout and never a drop passing his own lips. Seamus had made a promise to himself. He would never take the risk of being like his father.

Seamus took Annette to the club where he works. They caught the bus together. He didn't use his car for work, not ever. Fuel was expensive. Seamus had a budget that he had to adhere to, and it certainly didn't include using his car across London. Even in them days, income was small, and outgoings were big. England was a very chaotic place to be, by comparison to the the West of Ireland. Annette was astonished by the hustle bustle of London. So many people walking about. Motorcars everywhere. Loads of buses. Everywhere was so busy. Not at all like the sleepy village she has come from. Annette was lonely but she knew that there wasn't a choice for her, she had to leave her home in Ireland, but still, the memories of her mother's face when she gave her the news, will be in her mind, probably for a very long time. The wonderings of how Eefie is getting along without first her brother and now her sister. Annette wanted to cry. She knew that she couldn't because if she started she might not be able to stop. She would pinch herself, and positively look to her future. She would enjoy her time with her brother and finding out all about his new life in London. Maybe that she could make a new life too.

"Mammy and Daddy would be so proud of you Seamus; you play the flute so well. A musician in our family and they didn't even know".

Annette too liked London. She decided that she would stay for six months, maybe more, if she could find a job. She overheard a conversation between two girls talking in the club. The local hospital needs a new cleaner, and there's a room going too. Annette acted swiftly. The very next morning, she was up at the crack of dawn, got herself ready in quick sharp time, and took herself to the hospital. She told the manager

"I can work however many hours you need me too".

Annette enjoyed her job but was always conscious of the fact that she had the ability to do better things. Maybe she could do some training somewhere.

Eefie cried, and cried, when I left but what could I do? Daddy was still the same, always drinking, hitting us with the belt. Mammy tries but sure she's helpless. He's worked her into the ground. He beats her with his belt and his fists and pushed her down the stairs. Annette looked sad as she shared her thoughts with her brother. Daddy said that he will stop drinking, stop being a bully. He's made those promises so many times in the past and always lets himself down, lets his family down. Annette hadn't seen the change in her mother. She would be proud of her, she would also be proud of her father for the efforts that he is making. At last he won't see his children or his wife suffer any longer.

Attempted Reconciliation

They had been waiting almost two hours. The vet arrived as Padraig was leaving for the bogs. He had made himself some sandwiches and a bottle of tea. That's right! Padraig making his own sandwiches. He missed the way that Eileen made his lunches He wished for those days back. He did eventually accept that this was of his own making. That he had pushed his wife so far away, she no longer wanted to do things for him. A cow had been trapped in that dammed trench for 3 hours now. It's too late. The trenches are deep and not very wide. Another animal that they can't afford to lose.

"Jaysus Eileen we have to do something about getting those trenches filled in ".

Padraig wondered if maybe Michael could help.

"Kathy told me he's got some spare time next week. He could bring the digger and trailer. That way the job won't take too long. Will you ask him Eileen?"

Padraig was trying to engage the attention of his wife, in any way that he could. It wasn't working. He is going to have to work out a better plan.

Padraig had saved some money. It's been a long time since he put foot inside the door of Jimmy Donovan's public house. Now he uses some of his money to sort the vet's fees. He at last, can see that his marriage is over. That Eileen has lost all respect for him, in the same way that he lost respect for her many years ago. He is determined to do something about it. How can he get things back to where they were before, he wonders? He makes a plan! A padraig OShaunessey plan, is, probably a plan that will never come to fruition.

" We could go to see the priest. Have our vows renewed."

An excited Padraig spoke the words to his wife with a degree of enthusiasm but he should have known, should have realised that this wouldn't be enough

Oh my god, Eileen will need a little more, no a lot more, than the renewal of a vow, that they took all those years ago and Padraig didn't really live up to. All that's gone on since then and he thinks that a visit to the priest will make everything right again. The man's more stupid than I thought he was.

"It's no good Padraig. Just like the vet was too late, you're also too late. You have to get it into your head and accept what I'm telling you. Accept that our marriage is over, and that if, I never saw you again, it would be too soon. There's no turning back, it's done, and it's over".

Eileen felt that her words were harsh. She didn't feel comfortable in this conversation, but she realised that once and for all she had to be sure that her husband got the message

"As I said, I'm off to London to see our children, and you're not welcome".

"But the children. I too would like to see our children. And they, I'm sure would like to see me"

Eileen was aware, that there may have been some degree of truth in all of that. She wasn't going to allow that thought to interfere with her plans

"Jaysus Padraig after all you put me through, put us through, put the family through. A part of me has died inside. I have to be strong now and do what's right for me".

Eileen considered sharing her inner most thoughts with her husband. Sharing the feelings she has for another woman's husband. A woman who would be better suited to Padraig than to the man she's married to. She decided to keep her secret. Even if the revelation were to impact on Padraig in a way that made him look at his own actions a bit closer, it was still too late. Eileen would never again have trust in the man who destroyed her.

" You have to accept it Padraig. There's nothing left".

Eileen wiped a tear from her eyes.

"Jaysus Eileen you do care, look at ya, your crying, your upset".

Padraig really had little idea; he didn't really know his wife anymore. Eileen's tears were not for her husband and the loss of her marriage. Her thoughts were now deeply set on the day that Eamon had held her so close, had told her that she's the woman he loves. Her mind is absolutely made up, there's no going back now. Padraig made the tea. Two large cups taken from the special tea service given to them all those years ago as a wedding present. Padraig thought, that as they only come out on special occasions, it might melt Eileen's thoughts a little. He was wrong. They sat together in silence for the next ten minutes. Eileen then decided to once and for all, give her husband the news that he wouldn't want to hear. She wonders to herself if he will be straight back to O Donavan's. She decides that it's his responsibility and if he does, then so be it.

The Bad News for Padraig.

Eileen stood up as she began to speak; she remembered from her training days in Dublin, that the voice carries better, when the speaker is upright. She wanted the next thing she was going to say to have as big an impact as possible. She cleared her throat.

"I've got the tickets Padraig. Single only so there's no return date. The boats leaving in three weeks, and Eefies coming with me".

The colour drained from Padraigs face, he was distraught. He went to the floor on bended knees. He begged his wife for forgiveness. Promised that everything would be all right. What he didn't know about, of course, was his wife's feelings for another man. Her hopes for something to become possible between herself and Eamon O Hara.

She didn't hear Padraig, in fact, she was almost repulsed to see him on the floor, and she no longer cared. She had a sting in her voice, a voice that was usually gentle, and soft, but not now.

"You're pathetic Padraig, Get up "

She walked away and shut the door behind her. She went to the bottom room, where she sat, staring at the picture of our Lady, which was hanging on the wall. Eileen always talked to our Lady when in a difficult situation. She prayed for a few minutes. She didn't pray for her husband, or for their marriage to be reconciled. Eileen prayed that maybe one day she and Eamon could be together. She felt a surge of guilt, as she knew, that the only way for them to be together, would be in the event of the death of Padraig and Jackie. She consoled herself by reminding herself that she didn't ask for their death, she simply asked to be with Eamon, and after all she had put up with, and what Eamon puts up with, Jaysus don't they both deserve a little bit of happiness. The day that Padraig was dreading arrived. The clothes were neatly packed away in a small suitcase shared between them. Eileen had found a little compassion within her for her husband. She decided that if they appeared not to be taking too many belongings then he would get the feeling that it wouldn't be too long before they returned. Eileen made breakfast .Bacon and fried eggs for herself, a sausage for Eefie, fried till it was almost black just the way she like it.

"You should have some bread Eefie it's a long journey".

Padraig was outside milking the cows. He wasn't able to be in the same room as his wife and child this morning. Tears poured from his eyes almost as fast as the milk coming from the cow. Padraig knew that he had to get himself together. He couldn't let his daughter see how distressed he was feeling. Eefie was excited about her adventure. She was also worried for her father. How would he run the land, single hand? How would he cope on his own? Maybe Kathy and Michael would help him? Eileen tried to impress upon her daughter that those are adult concerns and not for her to be worrying about. Eileen reassured Eefie that they would be returning in a few months time and that the time would pass by real fast. Padraig made them all some tea and then took them to the train station, just like he took Eileen all those years ago when she was studying to be a doctor. Their lives flashed in front of them, remembering the way they held each other, all those years ago, when they were in love. Jaysus so much has happened since those days. The way that they loved each other and how they had created a child outside of their marriage and look at them now.

Eileen had longed for those days once more, but knew that it would never happen. She flinched at Padraigs attempt to caress her as she was boarding the train. Eefie held her father tightly she was brave she didn't cry. She wouldn't let her father see her inner distress. She gave him reassurance

"I love you daddy and we will be home soon"

Padraig, in his usual selfish way, made no attempt to disguise his emotions in front of his daughter. He made a last minute attempt to get something back from his wife.

"Jaysus Eileen we could get the old days back ".

She turned in silence. She sat down in what looked like, not the cleanest carriage on the train.

"Jaysus Eefie we could give ourselves a job here to pass the time "

The women laughed. The train pulled away. Eileen breathed a sigh of relief. At last she would have some space to think about her future, and the life she had shared with her bullying husband. Padraig watched the train in despair. He struggled with his own thoughts of, should he go to O Donovan's, or continue with a a sustained attempt to reconcile with his wife.

The train journey to Dublin seemed tedious for Eileen; she had done that journey so many times. Eefie was excited to be at the docks. She had never seen the sea before. She wondered how it would feel to be sailing. The crossing wasn't easy. The Irish sea was rough. Eileen and Eefie went up to the top deck. They stood quietly looking out at the waves. Every now and again Eefie felt a surge of nausea coming on

"Head down between your legs "

That was the best advice her mammy could give her. Eventually they arrived at Holyhead. Seamus and Annette were waiting for their mother and sister at the docks. Annette was very excited

" Seamus I can't bear it. It's been months and at last we are seeing mammy and Eefie again "

They waited anxiously for the planks to go down and for the moment when their mammy would walk off the boat. The time arrived. The O Shaunessey family were reunited, well almost. Eileen couldn't contain her emotions any longer. Firstly leaving her home, and the man that she had once loved and respected, and now seeing her two eldest children for the first time in months. She shed some tears

"Don't cry mammy "

Annette's voice was in a quiver as she hugged her mother. She wondered exactly what her mother's tears were for. The journey to London was long and tiresome. Eileen slept. Eefie was amazed at the sights. She had never seen so many cars together nor street lights. Eventually they all arrived at the place where Seamus now lives. He had arranged for the rent of an extra room. He had remembered how much his mammy adored flowers, and had placed a small flower arrangement on a shelf in the corner. The children had so much to say to each other.

"Eefie you've grown tall, so tall, in such a short time too".

Eefie became excited and wanted to share some news with her brother and sister

." Daddy's changed he's not drinking anymore and you'll never guess what else he does. No, you won't believe me!"

Seamus began to feel a little impatient. He wished that his sister would get on with her story. It wasn't going to be a nice story, how could it be? so let's get it over with. If it was about their father, and it supposedly was, then there would have to be, a but, or a maybe.

"Come on then Eefie spit it out; it's like waiting to have a tooth pulled "

Eefie took a deep breath before she began. She wanted to be sure that the words would come out right. She was feeling anxious that Seamus and Annette may not believe her.

"All right then, he goes bare hand fishing. Yes, he does Seamus, doesn't he mammy. Mammy tell him, tell him it's the truth."

Eileen could see the anguish in her daughters face. The need for everything to be all right between her parents. The desire from her daughter, for Eileen to say it's going to be ok. Could she do it for the sake of her children? Is it fair to herself? she deserves a life too?

In her wisdom Annette changed the subject.

"Mammy I'm working and I've got some money saved. I want to take you and Eefie to the Irish club. You can listen to Seamus playing the flute".

"Go away with ya, he doesn't play at the club surely"

"He does Mammy, tell her Seamus". Seamus decided to take his mother to the Irish club.

"Sure the craic is great. Everyone's so friendly, and there are some people from Roscommon who are looking forward to meeting you both".

Over the next few months, Eileen had occasional quiet periods, in order to consider her thoughts about her life back in Ireland. She enjoyed the time she was sharing with her children. She considered the implications to her family, should she decide not to return back to Padraig.

The local surgery somehow discovered that Eileen is a trained doctor. Had her children been manipulating situations in order to keep her in London? We know that Michael in particular didn't wish for his mammy to return in Ireland, so could this have been his doing? The surgery needed a temporary replacement. Dr Jones has been taken ill with pneumonia. The community doesn't have a doctor. Eileen has the experience. The invitation arrived in the post, she was surprised, to read that she was asked to go to the surgery for discussions the following Tuesday morning. Eileen wondered if she would have the confidence to take up the offer. She could certainly use the money it would bring in. She discussed this with her children, and after much deliberation, she spent the following six months, working five days a week, having weekends free to explore her new way of life. Seamus organised some dance nights, at the house he was living in. He provided the music. It reminded Eileen of her younger days when she and Padraig held house dances back in Ireland. Seamus has become a fabulous flute player and whilst this wasn't the usual venue for his music, he was happy to create entertainment for his mother, and the friends that she has made in London.

Eileen's thoughts during those months were rarely about her husband Padraig, except from the occasional wondering, of how he was doing with the drinking. Eileen found it difficult, not to show her feelings to her children, especially Eefie, who would constantly want to know

"Have you had a letter from daddy, how's he doing".

There had been letters, which were unopened. Eileen made the decision that she owed it to herself to have a time of peace and tranquillity. After all Padraig had created the situation. He had driven his children away, driven his wife away. Now, she wasn't going to engage in any knowledge of how he's currently living his life, and what will be, will be, was her new motto.

Eileen decided that she would talk to her children about her feelings. After all Padraig is their father. She knew that Seamus and Annette would understand the way things were. She wasn't sure about Eefie. She summoned her children to the kitchen

As Eileen began "Your daddy has been......She was abruptly interrupted by her daughter. Eefie had tears pouring from her eyes, and in between the sobs, she told them

" There are letters, I've seen them, and mammy hasn't opened them .I kept asking you about letters because I thought that it might make you feel guilty, and then you would open them, and find out what's happening to our daddy".

Eileen felt a sense of shock at the degree of deviousness and manipulation that was now coming from her youngest child. She hadn't reared her, to be this way. Eileen had to think quickly, she knew that she had to be strong, and if she ever had any intention of opening those letters, she couldn't do it now. She couldn't, she wouldn't be seen, to give in, to manipulation. That would not be in the interest of her daughter.

"Jaysus Eefie if the letters were addressed to you, then you would have had the rights to know what they contain, as they're not, you don't. You have disappointed me Eefie"

Eileen was stern in her voice.

" I don't appreciate your behaviour, and your tears, will have to be dealt with by yourself".

Eileen dismissed the meeting, and took herself for a very long walk. The park was so serene. In some ways it reminded Eileen of the fields back home. Now, probably for the first time since leaving, her head was seriously back in Ireland. She began to think seriously about Padraig. How they had once loved each other so much. How they have drifted apart. She wondered to herself if there could ever be reconciliation and if there were one, would it be for the right reasons. Eileen made a decision. She would write to Padraig. She would try to establish how he was living his life. Was he still off the booze or not? She would share her thoughts with her son. Seamus is mature; She knew that he would discuss the situation sensibly with her. She knew that he would not share the information with his sisters. Seamus was everything that his mother had hoped he would be. A caring young man with a maturity beyond his years. He was on the outside looking in. He did not want his mother to make further mistakes, by reconciling with their father for the sake of the children

"Jaysus ma, you've been battered and bruised by him. Take no notice of Eefie she doesn't understand, she's still a child. I've watched my Da behave like a drunkard and a brute for many a year.Ive grown up with him persecuting his own children for the mistake that he made. Jaysus how many times have I, have we, told him that Martins death was a simple accident that could have happened to anyone, a simple mistake that anyone could have made. That it was wrong to smother his other children because of Martin, and that if he didn't stop he would eventually lose all of us. He never listened, not really listened. He robbed you of your self esteem. How many years back in Ireland could you have worked as a doctor but wasn't able to because of him. I've watched you go down, and down, till eventually you made the break by coming to England. No Ma I don't hate him, nor treat him with contempt. He's still my father, and always will be, no matter what decision you make. You seem to be building a life for yourself here in London. Why would you want to go back to him, and doing it for others would never be right?"

Eileen decided to leave her thoughts right there, for now, and focus on other things. The weeks turned into months. She was gradually building up her new life. Working hard as a general practioneer. The surgery asked her to extend her contract for a further two years. She was delighted at the opportunity. This gave her the excuse, to tell her children that she is badly needed here, therefore she couldn't even think about her previous life back in Ireland, whilst she's so busy and so many people need her here in London. She watched her children grow and mature. Even Eefie had seemed to stop worrying about her father. This unknown to Eileen, may be due to the fact that Eefie had begun writing to him herself.

"Mammy can I talk to you? .Eefie looked anxious. There's a letter from daddy"

The colour drained from Eefies face. Eileen knew that it was going to be serious.

"He's sick. He's got cancer of the liver. He's been trying to tell you but you never opened his letters. I hate you, your letting our daddy die, and you don't even care".

Eileen wasn't surprised by the news. Sure how could he expect anything else after the way he has abused his body. Eileen had mixed feelings towards her daughter. She had sadness for her, in the knowledge, that she was as sure as anything can ever be, going to lose her father.

" Eefie come here".

Eileen's arms were wide open. Her daughter cried for what seemed like hours.

"I didn't mean it mammy. I don't hate you. I'm just so upset".

Eileen explained in the clearest way that she could, how the abuse of alcohol can and does affect a person's body, and in particular the liver. Her children understood. After much deliberation, and discussion, with Seamus in particular, the family decided to head back home to Ireland with immediate effect. The Irish club had a fundraising night. Seamus churned out the tunes on the flute. He was held in such high esteem at the club, once it was known that the event was to go towards an operation for his father, the customers started piling in to such an extent, that one fundraising night became three.

The journey home was tedious. Everyone slept, on and off, on the journey to Holyhead. The seats on the train were scruffy looking, with ripped blue covers. The windows very dirty, you couldn't see out. Eileen wished that there was a coffee machine, just like she did in her training days in Dublin many years ago. She wondered to herself if she might be going back there with Padraig. She hoped not. She didn't wish anything bad to happen to him. She almost began to allow herself to go back in her thoughts to the years when they first met. They were so much in love in them days, but now things are different. Padraig has created that situation by his behaviour, by his choice of life style. Yes, the family are now broken, and its Padraigs fault. Eileen decided that no matter how she finds her husband she will never forget that thought.

Eileen Returns Home to Ireland

Eventually they arrived at the docks at Hollyhead. Once the family had boarded the went to the restaurant. Perhaps some tea and a bite to eat would help settle the nerves. The sailing seemed to take an eternity. The sea was rough as usual. Eefie was sick for almost the whole of the journey. Eileen wondered if this was due to the rough waves, lashing back and forwards, or, was it Eefie being anxious, about how she would find her father. She would never really know the answer, but suspected that it was anxiety. Eefie remained fairly quiet throughout the journey. No one was certain what to expect, in regard to how they would find Padraig. Annette was especially anxious, as she hadn't seen her father for such a long time. Her eyes filled up with tears, her voice hardly recognisable

"Oh Mammy I'm so frightened, is Daddy going to die "?

The expression on Eileen's face must have given her some clues as to the severity of her father's illness. She was inconsolable for a short time, but then realised that she had to pull herself together. She couldn't allow her father to see her anxiety.

Eileen, being the usually selfless person that she is, and despite being overly tired from the long journey, put her daughter's feelings before her own needs. She hugged her daughter. She wiped the tears from her eyes. She gave words of encouragement to Annette about what a strong girl she is, and of how whatever happens to her father, she must know, that despite all his drinking habits, he always loved his children in his own way. Eileen wondered to herself about how convincing she was? She wasn't sure that she believed those sentiments herself, so how could she expect her child to believe them. Seamus had said little about their reason for going home. He was, on the whole, a quiet lad who didn't particularly show his emotions. Eileen knew him well enough though, to realise, that he would be thinking of his father, and remembering times gone by.

"It's going to be all right Seamus"

Her voice was quivering as she spoke the words she knew would not be the truth. Seamus could see his mammy's anxiety. He was wise enough to realise that Eileen no longer cared very much for Padraig. He didn't blame her for that. He had very vivid memories of his life growing up, and the way in which his father had behaved towards the whole family

Eileen bought a cheap car in Dublin, for them to use, for their time in Ireland. Seamus made the choice. He knew a little about cars. He decided that a beetle would be very suitable to meet their needs. They set off from

Dublin on the long journey to Mayo. There were many pretty villages to look at, as they drove through the narrow winding lanes. There were large statues of the Virgin Mary built into the side of the road in almost every village they passed through. They stopped at the road side about two hours from Mayo. Eileen was hungry. They ate sandwiches which had been bought in Dublin that morning. Eileen took some deep breaths. It was good to have the Irish air going in her lungs she thought. The drive to the old homestead seemed to go on and on. Seamus was such a bright and clever lad. He had no problem working out which way to go. The girls slept for part of the journey. The whole village were aware of their imminent return. Some tongues were no doubt bad mouthing the family. How could that Shaunnessey woman do it? How could she have just upped sticks and gone, and left that poor sick man? Little did they know that the sick man hadn't always been sick, well he had, but in a different way. Alcoholism is a sort of sickness, a very brutal one, that doesn't just affect the user, it affects the whole family. Heads would go down, whispering stopped, when they would see me appear. Kathy was at the house waiting. She had been helping Padraig. She was beside herself with excitement

"Oh my God Padraig they're here. It's Seamus driving a car, a small blue car with three doors. A beetle, I think. The first car probably to have ever been driven up to our home by a member of the O Shaunnessey family".

Kathy went running down the borreen, almost tripping over on the rough ground. She greeted them at the gates by the river. They all got out of the car to hug Kathy.

"Oh my god Eileen, you look amazing, and the children they have grown, and Seamus driving a car, a motor car, I can't believe it, everyone has changed so much"

Suddenly Kathy's expression changed, she became dull and gloomy looking.

"Its Padraig, he isn't too good. Jaysus Eileen I better warn you before you see him. Padraig hasn't been out of the house for weeks, in fact he's hardly been out of bed. Michael and I have been helping him on the land, but he absolutely refused to allow us to do anything in the house. It's not as you left it, not as you will remember it".

Once in the front door, Eileen recognised the stinch that was coming towards her. Many times in her medical practise in London and her training days in Dublin she had come across the odour of bed sores. She immediately knew, before even seeing Padraig that it wasn't going to be very good. The house looked rough. Dirty clothes, lay strewn in a pile, in one corner of the room. Unwashed crockery and cutlery in a bowl by the window. The whole place lacked a woman's touch. The grass in the front meadow was way over grown. Padraig was in his bed hardly able to move. He was delighted to see his family once more. He was so thin, so gaunt looking. His face expressed the immense pain that he was suffering. He was weak. Annette and Eefie were now by his side.

"You look well Da"

The words were strained as they tried to hold back the tears. They knew that Padraig didn't believe their words. How could he. His body was letting him down rapidly, but there was nothing wrong with his mind. The doctor had just been. Seamus and Eileen were still outside getting all the facts and information re the severity of Padraigs condition. The doctor's words seemed cold and callous

" Unless they have a miracle, it's going to be a matter of weeks. The plan to take Padraig to the hospital is in place. He will be more comfortable there. They should be able to do something to relieve the discomfort from the bed sores, as well as analgesic for the pain he's suffering".

Eileen was reassured and hoped that she would be able to offer some comfort to her children. She braced herself. Together with Seamus they went to Padraigs bedside. She had to be strong. She had to try to forget the past and how badly he had treated her and their children. If the children could forgive him, then she must too. She knew that her husband was dying. She would try to make his last weeks with the family, as comfortable as she possibly could do.

"It's good to see you Padraig, and to be sure, you're not looking too bad at all".

She leaned over, and kissed him on the forehead. Padraigs arm was outstretched towards his wife. His voice was weak and frail.

"Thank God that your here Eileen, and that you've brought the children". "

"Go away with you Padraig, sure you'll be up and about in no time at all .They're very good in that hospital you know, after all they trained me, so I'm the proof that they know what they're doing"

Padraig squeezed her hand, and smiled up at his son. Seamus put his ear near his father's mouth. He barely recognised the words that were being uttered. Padraig was making an attempt to tell his children how he regretted the restrictions he had placed upon them when they were growing up. Regretted the way he had beaten them, using the excuse that it was all about chastising. Seamus tried to be reassuring to his father

"Don't worry Da, you get some rest now, and when you're off to the bogs again, we will finish this conversation".

That was the way that Seamus had chosen, to refuse to hear the rubbish coming from his father's mouth without causing any further distress for anyone. Seamus and the girls had seen the strained look on their mothers face. Despite the fact that Eileen no longer felt anything for her husband other than contempt, he was still the father to her children. She would show him respect for that fact. Everyone, possibly including Padraig, knew that Padraig would never be going to the bogs again, or anywhere else for that matter, other than to the hospital. They watched the ambulance driving slowly along the lane, then up the borreen. Eileen knew that when it left with her husband inside, that this would in all probability be the last time he would travel along that lane.

Seamus and his mother travelled to Dublin by car. Eefie and Annette rode in the ambulance with their father. They enjoyed being able to comfort him, to loosen his clothing, to wipe his brow, to whisper in his ear.

"You'll be home in no time at all Da. It's amazing what treatments are available these days. Sure you'll be as good as new in a few weeks".

Padraig wondered if his daughters actually believed what they were saying. Later he confided in Eileen that he wished for them to know that he was a dying man. Wished for them to be strong and face the facts. Wished for them to understand that what was happening for him now was a result of his lifetime on the stout.

The journey to Dublin was a lengthy one. In some ways it reminded Eileen of her younger days, going there on the train. How strange it was for her to be back in the same hospital where she did her training all those years ago. Something's still looked the same. The nurses were still wearing the large blue hats that everyone complained about. They had a new cancer department now. Eileen was impressed. Padraig settled on the ward. The girls tried to hide their sniffles from him. They stayed at the hospital all day and actually a few hours into the night. Travelling home the following morning was tedious and tiresome. Eileen believed that she needed to be back home in order to meet her religious commitments.

Mass at eleven, on a Sunday morning, was still the order of the day at the local chapel. Eileen requested prayers, and a mass, to be said for her husband, to ease his suffering. She was usually a great believer in the power of prayer. She remembered her thoughts from long ago when she secretly wished to God that she and Eamon O Hara could be together. Those prayers were never answered. Eileen wondered if her prayers to reduce Padraigs pain would be answered either. Brendan O Hara was at Mass, together with his brother David and their parents. Jackie was seated in front of Eileen. Eamon on the opposite side. Why did the church impose this rule? Men opposite to Ladies! This surely was manmade, not god made, and made absolutely no sense at all to Eileen.

The meeting of the two families outside of the chapel was a little tense, a little strained. Jackie hadn't changed at all. Still appeared to be, not interacting with either of her children and not much different towards her husband. Jackie found it a strain to be polite; her words were tinged with harshness

"Jaysus sure your looking good Eileen"

Jackie forced a smile, as she flicked her long hair to one side. Only the best of clothes for her. She was wearing a deep Green coat, with brown winkle picker shoes, which had a small heel. Jackie was a tall lady, so didn't need the usual six inch stilettos.

"Padraigs dying. He's in the hospital in Dublin since last Tuesday".

Eileen's eyes welled up with tears. The children were serious looking, not even managing a smile for Brendan or David. Jackie remained cold in her response

"Well let's face it Eileen, he's been a drunk all his married life, so what can you expect, the liver will only take so much".

Eamon looked embarrassed with his wife's comments. He looked directly at Eileen. Immediately, both of them knew, that despite the fact that some years have passed since they last met, and despite the fact that Eileen's husband is on his death bed, the feelings of love and desire were still as strong as ever, between the two people who probably would never be able to be together.

"Eileen I'm so sorry for your bad news".

The words had a huge degree of sincerity, as Eamon wasn't the type of man to wish bad on anyone. Eefie wondered how Brendan was getting along. She remembered the days at school, when she would push him around the playground in his wheelchair. She remembered Eamon taking her home when she had the measles. She talked to Brendan in the knowledge that he probably didn't understand a single word. She did notice a smile though and that was good enough for her. Eefie reminisced

"You were so nice to me Eamon, giving me a ride home on the bicycle, when I had the measles. You were so nice to my mammy, when she was in the corner crying".

Eamon had a look of shock on his face .Eileen's heart went in her mouth. She had no idea, that her daughter had been aware of her crying, huddled in the corner, after Padraig had beaten her. Sweat began pouring from Eileen's brow. She wondered if her daughter had seen the hug between herself and Eamon, had she heard the conversation between them. ? Had she realised that they loved each other? She will probably never know the answers to her question, but felt that there was a high possibility that yes, Eefie did know those things. Eileen chuntered to herself. Well sure who could blame Eamon for being nice to me? Who could blame me for wanting something nice in my life?"

"Come on mammy, we have to go to Dublin. Seamus is waiting".

Eileen was becoming suspicious of everything now. She wondered if that was her daughter's way of getting her mammy away from Eamon, out of his company. Had Eeefie wished that the two families had never met? The hospital ward was unusually quiet. There were lots of empty beds. There was a curtain, now closed, around Padraigs bed. The matron called out to Eileen, just in time, before she opened the curtain.

" Father John has been Eileen; he got here just in the nick of time. Padraig went very peacefully. He took a turn for the worst during the night then he drifted off to sleep and simply didn't wake up. The matron tried to be reassuring; he passed away, very, very peacefully"

Eileen had to hold her daughters back.

"We want to see him mammy"

Seamus had been to park the car. He could now see from the expression on his families face that something bad had happened.

"Has he gone. Is he dead "?

Seamus was cold in his tone. I suppose that this reflected his feelings in regards to his upbringing from his father.

"Come on Seamus"

Eefie extended her arm. She took hold of her brother's hand. She pulled him towards her and they had a hug. There were no tears from anyone now. It was almost, as if their tears had been cried, throughout their life, living with Padraig. Eileen and her children went out of the hospital, over the road to the small chapel. They prayed for the repose of the soul of their dead father and husband. Eileen used to visit that Chapel when she was living in Dublin as a student doctor. They went back to the hospital once more. Eileen wanted to say "Thank you" to the nursing staff, and to a young doctor, whom she had been told was in the early stages of her training. Eileen had remembered her own training days and seeing the first corpse, and how difficult that had been for her. She wanted to thank the student doctor who had been with her husband, and to give her the reassurance that it does get easier as you progress through your training.

The journey home from Dublin was a very quite one. Not a word spoken between them. Even Seamus didn't have a stop to stretch his legs. The body was brought from Dublin in a funeral car, and kept at the house for four days. Neighbours called to pay their respects. Some had remembered Padraig from his younger days when he had lived the life of a very decent man. Woodbines were passed round on a silver tray. The morning for the funeral arrived. Eileen and the children were very brave. Padraigs coffin was carried up the borreen by his Son Seamus and five other men from adjoining villages. The cart was laden, this time, to carry Padraig to the cemetery where the priest said mass. It was the same priest who refused to marry Eileen and Padraig all those years ago. He seemed like a very old man now. Eileen wondered if he had opened his mind any more to the ways of the world. The funeral procession went in part along the road, and in part over the fields. Padraig had liked going to the Chapel using both ways. As this was his last journey Eileen attempted to do it as she felt he would have wished. The mass seemed to go on forever more, then onto the cemetery for burial. A small reception was being held in Donovan's that afternoon and evening. A request came from Jimmy Donovan to Seamus to go to the bar for a private chat. Jimmy handed Seamus an envelope

"Your father gave this to me. He said that I should give it to you after his death"

With shaking hands Seamus opened the envelope. There was a small piece of paper inside. Read it then Seamus his sisters were getting anxious.

"To my children and my dear wife I will be in the graveyard when you open this letter. I am truly sorry for the suffering that I have caused for you all. I never managed to forgive myself, for the death of our son, your brother Martin. I do know that you have all made good lives for yourselves. I do know Seamus that you are a great musician. In fact I always knew but couldn't tell you that I knew, because I couldn't bear to hear you playing the flute when Martin couldn't be here to enjoy

229

it. Yes I agree, that makes me a very selfish man. My last and dying wish is that when you have read this letter that Seamus would play a few reels, and jigs, right here in Donovan's bar right now. That you all might celebrate my life and not mourn my death".

"Go on Seamus it's what Daddy wanted"

The words came from Annette with a quivering voice. Seamus looked at his mother for her approval. Eileen nodded. Jimmy brought out a flute from the back room. Even Eileen joined in with the dancing, and that was the end of Padraigs life on this earth.

Eileen leaves for London Again

The time seemed right for Eileen to move on with her life. She had made her mind up very clearly that she would never return to Ireland to live back in the house. At that point, she returned to London with her children. She had some time out from her work in order to sort her head. Eventually she took up her previous position as the local doctor. The practise was delighted to have her back

"Jaysus Eileen it's great to meet you"

The accent and the expression gave it away. He was another doctor from our green land that crossed the ocean to make a better life.

"All the patients keep asking for you Eileen. You're very popular the receptionist told her. You remember old Mr Franklyn, you know, the gentleman with the gangrenous leg, well, he came into the surgery last week, hopping along",

"Where's Doctor O Shaunessey. He was agitated in his voice. There was no pacifying him; he wanted to see Eileen and no one else. It was the same with many of the patients".

Eileen brought new ideas and a fresh look on medicine, to the practise. She started up a small clinic for new mothers, where they could bring their babies. She brought lots of enthusiasm to the practise and worked very long hours. Her fellow Irish man had demonstrated a keen interest in her. He was a widower and had been so, for about six years.

"I lost my wife to cancer. I've never remarried in fact I've never been out with another woman. I hear that you're a widow Eileen, jaysus it's hard "

His words echoed in her head throughout the evening. Eileen comes from good stock. She has never been a defeatist. She found solutions, not problems. This would not defeat her now. She would move on with her life. Over the next few months, she thought a lot about her life back in Ireland. She thought a lot about Eamon O Hara, and what her life might have been like, had she had the good fortune to have fallen in love with him, in the beginning, instead of Padraig O Shaunessey. Eamon was supporting her in terms of her pursuing her career. He had organised the letting of her land. A neighbour, paid twenty pounds rent for a six month period. The cows would keep the grass down. There was an income generated from that, and the place would still be there in years to come, if she ever decided, that she would like to settle in Mayo. Eileen was delighted to hear the news that her two older children were settling down in their lives. Seamus had met a girl from Cork. Her name is Noreen, and they cared deeply for each other. Noreen had lived in London for almost one year now. It wasn't the same culture shock for her, as it had been for Seamus. Cork even in those days, was quite a large city, well certainly in respect and comparison to where Seamus had originated from. She is a student nurse on work experience at the practise where Eileen works, and very much the marrying kind. They would have seven children, or so her grandmother had always told her. She's nineteen, but more like a twenty five year old. Noreen is a tall girl with long fair hair and pretty blue eyes. She and Seamus met at the club where he works. She also loves traditional Irish music and plays the button accordion herself.

"Be away with you Seamus, sure if I ever give up on nursing, we can join together as a duet, or maybe even join an Irish band here in Camden Town".

Both Seamus and Noreen are sensible people with very bright futures ahead of them. It was therefore a great surprise to them both, when they discovered that Noreen was going to have a baby.

"Jaysus Noreen how did we let this happen? We have always been so careful; it must have been a faulty one".

Seamus was annoyed with himself. Their future no longer seemed so bright.

" What will your parents say? What will my ma say? Her being a doctor and all that, maybe she will want to help you get rid of it?"

Noreen was visibly distressed by her boyfriend's reaction. She too felt that now everything in their lives would change but couldn't bear to hear the words get rid of it. She would have this baby and people will have to deal with it. Eileen was furious with her Son and with Noreen also.

"There's no excuse Seamus. There is contraception fairly readily available. You're not in Ireland you know".

Eileen was not taking the moral high ground. She was however hugely disappointed, as she could see the implications to their life's, and how this would have an impact on Noreen's career in particular. She took a long walk in order to think things through carefully. She remembered her own first pregnancy and how she didn't allow it to interfere with her career. She sat for what seemed like ages on a bench in the local park. Later that evening she decided to visit Seamus. She requested that Noreen be present also.

"Jaysus Seamus you know how angry she was, she's going to be talking about abortions, and all that, or maybe even adoption"

Eileen arrived at the flat. Seamus thought about how calm, and serene she looked, unlike the last time he saw her, when she had a look of a mad woman.

"It's nice to see you Mammy Noreen's making the tea".

Eileen told them both that she had been thinking. Thinking about her own past and how things had worked out for her. Seamus wondered what she was talking about. Eileen began to explain about her own younger years, when she had been in love with his father Padraig O Shaunessey. The colour drained from Seamus face .He got a shock. He had no idea that his mammy had a shotgun wedding. That his deceased brother Martin was conceived out of wedlock

"What in Holy Ireland"

He was in disbelief. After sharing the information with Noreen and Michael, Eileen reassured them both that she would help out over the following months and that she would help Noreen to get back into her nursing career if that's what she wanted .Noreen's pregnancy was quite similar to Eileen's. The difference was at the end. Noreen's baby was born in a maternity home in Camden Town. She had been given some pain relief and made to feel as comfortable as could be possible. Noreen gave birth to a baby boy. Eileen had her first grandchild, and I was a great grandmother. Michael and Noreen will be married in a few years time. They will marry for the right reasons

Eileen asked me to go to England, to meet the new baby. Kathy and Michael were going for a short visit. I could travel with them. I wasn't sure.

"Jaysus Eileen I'm getting old you know".

"Come on mammy, sure it will do you good. You could come over at Christmas time and see the difference in this country. London lights up, sparkly trees everywhere. You can see Seamus playing at the club".

I decided I would go. Eileen organised the tickets for the train and the sailing. We all left together; however, Kathy and Michael would return two weeks before me. They couldn't leave the land unattended for too long. The day of departure arrived. I was feeling excited, tinged with anxiety for many different reasons. The car came to take us to Balla. As we drove down the boreen I wondered if I would ever return, or if this might be the last time I would see my birth place. I hadn't told anyone about the chest pain that keeps coming back. Each time, I wonder if it's going to take my last breath. We left Balla on the train at two o clock in the afternoon. In fact, this was my first ever train journey. I didn't know what to make of it, and how was I going to cope with the sailing. I had never before in my life been out of Mayo, and now I was on my way to England. As we travelled across Ireland to reach Dublin, I was in awe of all the pretty villages, some with what I considered to be very posh looking houses. I remembered my late husband John. I wondered what he would make of it all. We arrived at the docks two hours before time for departure. Kathy had packed some sandwiches and a bottle of tea each. The weather was very cold. There was frost on the ground and we were expecting snow. We found a small empty room near the docks where we sat and ate our sandwiches. We boarded the ship, at half past six in the evening, and arrived in Holyhead at one in the morning. Eileen came to meet us. She was driving now. This was also a first visit to England for Michael and Kathy. Christmas was wonderful. I managed to see many new and different things and places. I fell in love with my new grandchild. I could sense that John was there. Oh how I longed for him, again and again, and again. The weeks went by very quickly, leading up to the point where I was going back to Ireland. Eileen and I had some time alone at a little cafe on the high street in Camden Town Eileen began to reflect on her past

"Jaysus mammy, how things have changed, how the times have changed. "

In my day, you couldn't possibly be an unmarried mother, well not in holy Mayo anyhow. I wondered how Eileen was really feeling about the whole situation. In many ways she is so like me. I thought that perhaps she wouldn't show her true feelings if she considered that it may be hurtful to her child. I had been wrong about that.

"Jaysus mammy I was furious with them both and I told them so"

We finished the conversation and the tea and had a short walk to the bus stop which would take us back to Eileen's home. The following day we set out on the journey back to Holyhead and then the sailing to Ireland. I was apprehensive. Would I be all right on my own? Eileen was very reassuring

"Its easy mammy I will put you on the ship and when you come out of the docks at Dunlaire there will be a car from Balla to meet you . You will see it plainly. It's the same car, same driver, that picked you up to take you to Ballagh".

Eileen had thought of everything. As Eileen said her goodbyes, she wondered if this might be the last time she would see her mother alive. She hoped not, and prayed to Our Lady, for another family gathering, which would include her mammy the following Christmas. I slept for most of the sailing and in no time at all I was in the car on the last stretch of the journey home. I arrived back in my own home on the evening of the twenty seventh of January.

Annette has met a young man from Camden town, right there in London. They too had marital plans in place.

"Mammy meet James"

The introductions went very well.

"I've heard lots about you Mrs O Shaunessey. Annette's been telling me all about growing up in Mayo and life on the farm".

James had an Irish Brogue himself, and had Eileen play the guessing game. She had no idea really where he might be from. Eventually, he told her, that he originated from Kilkenny Town. That his father was a hospital consultant, and had spent many years working in Dublin, in some hospital or other there. Eileen's thoughts went back to Gerry Corcoran. She wondered if it could be too much of a coincidence that it be the same person she had worked with all them years ago. She asked James if he had a good upbringing, a good family life. James was a little hesitant in his response.

"Well, Mrs O Shaunessey, It was like this"

James told her, about how he and his sister had been raised to the age of eleven, and thirteen, by an Aunt. His mammy had been an alcoholic and his Da working away. James explained that to his amazement, one day some years ago now, his father returned back To Kilkenny, to work at the hospital there. He told his family, that he had met a young student doctor in Dublin. He had shared with her some information about his family life. She told him that he should move back to Kilkenny and sort things out. James went on to say, that as a family, they are forever indebted to that young doctor. That It's because of her understanding, and guidance to his father, that their family have been reunited, that their mammy got help with her alcohol addiction. Eileen remembered Gerry Corcoran very well, she knew that he had to be James's father, but for absolute confirmation, she asked young James for his last name. Eileen wondered, yet almost knew the answer to the question she was about to ask herself. Did Gerry Corcoran ever tell his family how he got to be having that conversation with the young doctor in Dublin? Eileen felt a great sense of achievement, in the knowledge, that when she as a young girl, she had the opportunity to date a prestigious member of the hospital team. She turned him down because, it would have been morally wrong. Wrong for her because she was in love with Padraig O Shaunessey and because she had been informed that Gerry was a married man. Instead she had put him in his place, and sent him on a journey that she now knows brought his family back together. Will she ever divulge to young James or to her daughter Annette, that she was the doctor who had helped James's family? Annette and James were due to be married the following year. James had been given some money from his father .He would invest it in a property just outside of Camden Town. A small house with three bedrooms, two lounging rooms and a neat front garden. James and Annette both studied for, and now practise Physiotherapy. They both have jobs at the local hospital, however their plan is, that if, and when, they have a family of their own, Annette, would be able to open a private practise and run it from their home.

Their journey, from that first meeting, to where they are today, has been a turbulent one in many ways.

Some months after they first met, James had been stricken down with a stomach infection. In the beginning, the feeling was that it was a bug, nothing more serious than that. After several days of vomiting and bowel problems his body began to collapse. Annette called the ambulance. James was admitted to the hospital where he remained for the following eight months. During those months, he encountered the ultimate indignity. He became doubly incontinent and unable to do any personal care. Annette was devastated, but continued to be a rock in the relationship. She has a very strong sense of character. They both have a great belief in their Catholic Faith and prayed fervently for a recovery. This is what saw her and James through those dreadful weeks, leading up to a clinical diagnosis. The future was very uncertain for them. The whole of James's nervous system had been attacked .There were question marks surrounding whether he would eventually make a full recovery or not. Eileen had been a source of strength to them. She was able to reassure ,that she had seen patients in that position who had moved on ,mostly getting their life back to about 95% of where it was before the illness. This wasn't good enough for James; he also had a great strength of character and determination. He pushed himself, where others, may well have given up.

"Jaysus Annette I'm not letting this beat me"

James went from strength to strength. Each passing week brought new areas of progress, until he was eventually let out of the hospital, with the aid of a wheelchair, then progressed on to a walking stick, until eventually he made a full recovery. James and Annette practise physiotherapy in that same hospital which took him through those turbulent times.

Eileen often wondered about her youngest daughter and the possibility of her finding herself a husband in the future. She did go out at the weekends. She never brought any boys to meet her mother. Annette told her mammy that she shouldn't worry. She should remember that Eefie could be quite secretive reminding her mammy about the letters from Padraig and how Eefie hadn't told anyone.

Eamon and Jackie continued with their lives in their usual manner. Eamon continued to enjoy his job at the local school and being a main carer for his son Brendan. Eamon was fully aware that Brendan would always need special care and as he got older this was becoming harder for Eamon to meet his needs as well as doing a demanding job. Jackie didn't get any more graceful with age. She never developed a genuine interest in her children, or in her husband for that matter. She must have asked herself the question

"Why did she ever bother to have children?"

She continued to take trips away especially to New York. It was on one of those trips, that another family suffered the loss of a parent. Jackie was travelling across New York to visit her Aunt Kathleen. The train was crammed. It was winter time. Snow was falling thick and heavy. Visibility was poor. A herd of cows had broken free from a farmer's field which was at the side of the rail tracks. They wandered onto the track. The force of the impact threw some passengers from their seats. Jackie was one of those people. She sustained a fatal blow to her head. Death was sudden, so it was reassuring, for the family to have the knowledge that she didn't suffer. When Kathleen was given the news of her Nieces death, she insisted that she would make all the arrangements to have the body flown back to Ireland. She would pay all the costs with no expense spared. Kathleen remembered her first meeting, some years ago when her Niece had focused so much on herself. Kathleen was glad that she had stood up to her, and had wondered if Jackie had become any more involved in the life's of her children and in particular in Brendan's life

Eamon was at school when the telegram arrived. The colour drained from his face. Poor Eamon, his thoughts were not for himself, not even for his wife, who has just lost her life, but for his children, who he knew adored their mother despite her not feeling the same towards them, and towards Brendan in particular. Eamon dreaded that evening. He would have to tell David. How would he take the news? How would he get Brendan to understand? He would have to enlist some help from someone, from somewhere. Eamon was an only child. Both his parents were now deceased. Jackie was also an only child and both her parents now deceased. There wasn't any blood family. No one to turn to. Eamon shivered uncontrollably at the thought of what the evening would bring. Kathy and Michael Mc Geever were the closest thing that he had to family. He felt close to Kathy through his love for her sister. Kathy was stunned to hear the news.

"Jaysus Eamon come and sit down will ya"

Michael came in from the bogs. They all left to go to Eamons home to give the news to his children. A stunned silence surrounded the house. Brendan suddenly had a fit of laughter. It lifted the mood a little. At least he didn't have to know what has happened to his mammy. David asked lots of questions with a maturity that you wouldn't have expected from someone of his age. A second funeral took place in the village. The procession was small. Jackie had not been particularly loved by anyone. There were no celebrations of her life, nor no mourning her death, after the burial. Her husband, simply took his family back home, and attempted to get on with their lives, in the best way that he could. Eamon wished with all his heart that Eileen was there with him. She would know what to do, know how to sort Brendan out. He wanted to be in her arms and have her in his. He knew that this wouldn't happen, after all, they did have the Irish Sea between them.

The following months saw Eamon taking some time off from his teaching post. Brendan had become more and more challenging as time went by. He really hadn't known where his mammy was. He was used to her going away, but never for such a lengthy period of time. David tried to support his father as best he could. Juggling studying at the local college, with fairly regular trips over to England didn't leave a great deal of time for much else. David was a quiet young man. He didn't like to share his life events with anyone and least of all with his father. David would be an accountant one day. He had always enjoyed mathematics when he was at school. Balla needed a good accountant he was going to be it.

The surprise for Eamon was immense, when David announced to him, that Eefie O Shaunessey would be returning back to Ireland together with her mother. David told his father that he and Eefie had been in love for a very long time. That plans were partially laid. That there would be a wedding and it would be right here in the O Shaunessey household.

Some weeks later Eileen arrived back home, together with her youngest daughter. She was met at the bridge by Eamon O Hara

"Oh my god, Jaysus Eamon I'm so sorry for your bad news. I'm so sorry that you lost Jackie".

Eileen was insincere in her speech. How could she possibly be anything else, when she was in love with Eamon herself, and she knew that he loved her too? They fell into each other's arms for what seemed like an eternity. Eileen and Eamon, once they recovered from the news of their children getting married to each other, were thrilled in the knowledge that they had a job ahead of them which they would have to share. A wedding had to be planned. The house had to be prepared. Seamus and Noreen would come home for the wedding. They would provide the music. Annette was going to be a bridesmaid. It was all falling into place. The biggest shock of all was yet to come. Eefie had been secretively discussing things with David and Eamon. She was delighted with their response. Eefie had known all along how much Eileen and Eamon loved each other. She wanted her mammy to have some happiness in her life. She talked to her Aunt Kathy about her feelings, about her plan for her mammy and Eamon.

Eamon got down on his Knee in front of their children. The double wedding was the best celebration in this village, since the party many years ago, for Eileen's new post as the local doctor. Eileen has now returned to live in the home place, together with her second husband and his Son Brendan

I know that Johns watching over them and will give them guidance in a spiritual way. I know that he would be so proud of all of his family. I am the happiest that I have been for many a year. I know that my daughter is married to a good man, a gentle man who will love and respect her till the day she dies.

This manuscript was found by Eefie O Hara, (Nee Shaunessey), on the morning that she went into her Grandmothers room, to move out the belongings, after her grandmother's death. The composition was in a sealed envelope in the cupboard in the top corner of the room. It was marked

"For my grandchildren, Seamus, Annette and Eefie. For my daughters Eileen and Kathy. For my sons-in-law Michael and Eamon. Between you all, you have made my life very happy, very special and very complete. Also remembering my late husband John and late son-in-law Padraig O Shaunessey, whom I will have joined, by the time that you're reading this".

About The Author

Beatrice Finn was raised in a small village named Derrinabroock in Cloontia. She lived there for the first fourteen years of her life. Starting school at the age of seven years , Beatrice had a basic education. Her broader education came from the experience of living on a farm, up to the point of emigration to England with her family.

Beatrice has extended her education, within her career as a support worker in the NHS. More recently as a foster carer, fostering challenging teenagers for the Local Authority.

Beatrice has had a short article published in the past. This is her first attempt at writing a novel

Printed in Great Britain
by Amazon.co.uk, Ltd.,
Marston Gate.